北大社"十三五"职业教育规划教材

高职高专物流专业"互联网+"创新规划教材

物流专业英语
（第3版）

仲　颖　王　慧 ◎ 主　编
丛　倩　高晓英 ◎ 副主编

内 容 简 介

本书是高职高专物流管理专业英语教材，全书共 12 个单元，涉及物流的基本概念、供应链管理、物流运输、库存管理、物流包装、配送管理、绿色物流、物流单证等物流管理的各个方面。每个单元由导入案例、课文和阅读材料等组成，并设置巩固练习题供学生练习。本书内容结合物流案例、物流游戏、物流新闻、物流单证和物流前沿趋势等讲解，内容生动，词汇基础，适合教师教学和学生自学。

本书可作为高职高专物流管理、国际货代及相关专业的专业英语教材，也可作为物流行业从业人员的参考阅读资料或培训教材。

图书在版编目 (CIP) 数据

物流专业英语 / 仲颖，王慧主编 . —3 版 . —北京：北京大学出版社，2022.1
高职高专物流专业"互联网 +"创新规划教材
ISBN 978-7-301-32728-9

Ⅰ. ①物… Ⅱ. ①仲…②王… Ⅲ. ①物流—英语—高等职业教育—教材 Ⅳ. ① F25

中国版本图书馆 CIP 数据核字 (2021) 第 235446 号

书　　　名	物流专业英语（第 3 版） WULIU ZHUANYE YINGYU（DI-SAN BAN）
著作责任者	仲　颖　王　慧　主编
策 划 编 辑	蔡华兵
责 任 编 辑	蔡华兵
数 字 编 辑	金常伟
标 准 书 号	ISBN 978-7-301-32728-9
出 版 发 行	北京大学出版社
地　　　址	北京市海淀区成府路 205 号　100871
网　　　址	http://www.pup.cn　新浪微博：@ 北京大学出版社
电 子 信 箱	pup_6@163.com
电　　　话	邮购部 010-62752015　发行部 010-62750672　编辑部 010-62750667
印 刷 者	三河市北燕印装有限公司
经 销 者	新华书店
	787 毫米 × 1092 毫米　16 开本　11.75 印张　285 千字
	2011 年 1 月第 1 版　2017 年 1 月第 2 版
	2022 年 1 月第 3 版　2023 年 7 月第 2 次印刷
定　　　价	39.00 元

未经许可，不得以任何方式复制或抄袭本书之部分或全部内容。
版权所有，侵权必究
举报电话：010-62752024　电子信箱：fd@pup.pku.edu.cn
图书如有印装质量问题，请与出版部联系，电话：010-62756370

PREFACE 第 3 版前言

物流管理（logistics management）是指为了以合适的物流成本达到用户满意的服务水平，对正向及反向的物流活动过程及相关信息进行的计划、组织、协调与控制。物流专业英语是在英语环境下培养具备基本物流管理能力的人才，使其掌握物流管理的最新动态，能进行物流英语的专业表述和实际应用。

党的二十大报告指出，加快发展物联网，建设高效顺畅的流通体系，降低物流成本。随着经济的不断发展，物流在我国社会经济生活中的作用越来越重要，与之相应的物流学科的有关内容也在不断地发展。掌握一定的物流专业英语词汇，有助于提高物流专业水平。物流专业英语是一门综合性很强的课程，应用范围非常广泛，可以让学生在英语环境下理解物流的基本概念、体验物流的工作流程、设计物流的项目场景、模拟物流的工作环境等。本书就是为了培养全面化的物流专业人才而推出的。

本书在第 2 版的基础上修订而成，对部分阅读材料进行了调整，对全书语法和词汇进行了梳理，还进行了版式调整，以使全书内容更加适合教学和阅读需要。本书编写遵循工学结合、模拟场景等人才培养模式的改革导向和教学过程"实践性、开放性和职业性"的改革重点要求，在选材上力求紧贴物流学科的发展趋势，反映现代物流的热点问题。

本书内容可按照 48 学时安排教学，每个单元 4 学时。用书教师可根据不同的专业需要灵活安排学时，课堂重点讲解每个单元的主要内容，灵活地采用案例导入、话题讨论、学生演示、角色设计、模拟场景等教学方法；每单元相关练习可由学生在课后完成。

本书由江苏海事职业技术学院仲颖、王慧担任主编，由南京科技职业学院丛倩、江苏海事职业技术学院高晓英担任副主编。其他参编人员有南京交通职业技术学院余霞、陈乃源，无锡商业职业技术学院钟茂林，南京铁道职业技术学院尹新，以及江苏海事职业技术学院简耀、韩蕙、朱莉蓉、纪越。全书由仲颖统稿。

本书具体编写分工为：仲颖编写 Chapter 1 和 Chapter 9，丛倩编写 Chapter 2，丛倩、纪越编写 Chapter 3，钟茂林、纪越编写 Chapter 4，钟茂林、韩蕙编写 Chapter 5，王慧、简耀编写 Chapter 6，余霞、简耀编写 Chapter 7，陈乃源编写 Chapter 8，朱莉蓉编写

Chapter 10，高晓英编写 Chapter 11，尹新编写 Chapter 12。

  本书在编写过程中，参考了一些相关的文献资料，听取了许多行业资深人士的宝贵意见，在此谨向对本书的编写、出版提供帮助的人士表示衷心的感谢！

  由于编者水平有限，编写时间仓促，书中难免存在不妥之处，敬请广大读者批评指正。本书提供参考译文、参考答案，读者可联系编辑索取。

编 者

2021 年 6 月

CONTENTS 目 录

Chapter 1 Logistics Management — / 1

    Case Study   Walmart Wins with Logistics / 1
    Text A   What Is Logistics? / 4
    Text B   Develop Systems Visibility to Material Shipment / 7
    Reading Material A   P.G. Logistics / 11
    Reading Material B   GM Develops Vector as Its Fourth Party
        Logistics Provider / 12
    Reading Material C   Cold Chain Introduction / 15

Chapter 2 Supply Chain Management — / 16

    Case Study   Beer Game and Bullwhip Effect / 16
    Text A   Introduction to Supply Chain Management / 20
    Text B   Top 8 Biggest Supply Chains / 23
    Reading Material   Blockchain Used to Track Cashmere Supply Chain / 26

Chapter 3　Transport Management / 28

　　Case Study　The Snakes and Ladders Game / 28
　　Text A　History of Transport / 31
　　Text B　Transportation Elements / 33
　　Text C　Transportation Mode / 36
　　Reading Material　Improved Safety and Performance at Lower Cost / 41

Chapter 4　Inventory Management / 43

　　Case Study　Why Does an Inventory Error Affect Two Periods? / 43
　　Text A　Introduction of Inventory / 45
　　Text B　Principles of Inventory / 51
　　Reading Material A　JIT Inventory Management / 56
　　Reading Material B　New Trend of Inventory Management / 59

Chapter 5　Warehouse Management / 61

　　Case Study　Public Bonded Warehouse / 61
　　Text A　Types of Warehousing / 62
　　Text B　Warehouse Equipment / 67
　　Reading Material A　Web Firms Go on Warehouse Building Boom / 73
　　Reading Material B　VMI Technical Implementation Plan / 75

Chapter 6　Packaging Management / 77

　　Case Study　IKEA Changed the Packaging of Tea Candle / 77
　　Text A　The Importance of Packaging in Logistics / 80

Text B　Packaging Helps to Optimize Logistics Units　　　　　　　/ 84
Reading Material　Green Packaging Management of
　　Logistics Enterprises　　　　　　　　　　　　　　　　　　　/ 88

Chapter 7　Distribution Management ——————— / 91

Case Study　Distribution Management:
　　Control and Collaboration from Supplier to Customer　　　　　/ 91
Text A　Concept of Distribution Management　　　　　　　　　　/ 93
Text B　Public and Private Warehouses　　　　　　　　　　　　　/ 97
Text C　Physical Distribution　　　　　　　　　　　　　　　　　/ 102
Reading Material　Logistics Distribution + Consumption Upgrading
　　and Mode Innovation　　　　　　　　　　　　　　　　　　　/ 105

Chapter 8　Green Logistics ————————————— / 107

Case Study　Good for the Environment, Good for Business　　　　/ 107
Text A　Green Logistics　　　　　　　　　　　　　　　　　　　/ 109
Text B　Reverse Logistics　　　　　　　　　　　　　　　　　　/ 114
Reading Material　A Blueprint for Green Logistics　　　　　　　　/ 120

Chapter 9　Integrated Logistics ———————————— / 123

Case Study　Supply Chain Integration Becomes a Reality　　　　　/ 123
Text A　Integrated Logistics　　　　　　　　　　　　　　　　　/ 125
Text B　The Integrated Model of FedEx Corporation　　　　　　　/ 129
Reading Material A　Integration Meets Resistance　　　　　　　　/ 133
Reading Material B　Major Food Safety Risks in China's Supply Chain / 134

Chapter 10 Logistics Documents / 137

  Case Study   FedEx Trade Networks for Cargo Insurance / 137
  Text A   Electronic Delivery of Documents / 139
  Text B   Letter of Credit / 142
  Text C   Bill of Lading / 147
  Reading Material   Logistics Documents in Practice / 152

Chapter 11 International Logistics / 156

  Case Study   A Reliable Partner of P&G on International Logistics / 156
  Text A   Concepts of International Logistics / 159
  Text B   The Factors That Influence International Logistics / 162
  Reading Material   Leading Companies Operating in the International Logistics Industry / 166

Chapter 12 Logistics Business Correspondence / 170

  Case Study   Specimen Letter about Claim for Improper Packing / 170
  Text A   Introduction to Logistics Business Correspondence / 171
  Text B   Establishing Business Relations / 175
  Reading Material   Response to Complaints and Claims / 180

参考文献 / 181

Chapter 1
Logistics Management

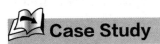 **Case Study**

Walmart Wins with Logistics[①]

Kmart and Walmart were two **retail merchandise chains** that, a few years ago, looked alike, sold the same products, sought the same customers, and even had similar names. When the race

---

① logistics [ləˈdʒɪstɪks]　　n. 后勤；物流；组织工作　　根据《中华人民共和国国家标准 物流术语》(GB/T 18354—2021)，物流是指根据实际需要，将运输、储存、装卸、搬运、包装、流通加工、配送、回收、信息处理等基本功能实施有机结合，使物品从供应地向接收地进行实体流动的过程。

began, people were quite familiar with the "big red K", whose stores **dotted metropolitan** areas but few had heard of Walmart, whose stores were in **rural** settings. **Considering** the similarity of the stores and their **mission**, **analysts attribute** the fates of the two chains **primarily to** differing management **philosophies**.

In 1987, Kmart was far ahead, with twice as many stores and sales of US $26 billion, compared to US $16 billion for Walmart. With its **urban presence** and a focus on advertising, Kmart had more **visibility**. In contrast, Walmart began in **stand-alone** stores outside small towns, luring customers away from the stores in **aging downtown**.

Kmart **executives** focused on **marketing** and **merchandising**, even using Hollywood star Jaclyn Smith to promote her clothing line. By contrast, Sam Walton, Walmart's founder, was **obsessed** with operations. He invested millions of dollars in a company-wide computer system linking cash registers to **headquarters**, **enabling** him to quickly **restock** goods. He also invested heavily in trucks and modern **distribution centers**. Besides **enhancing** his control of the supply chain, these moves sharply reduced costs. While Kmart tried to improve its image and **cultivate** store **loyalty**, Walmart kept lowering costs, betting that price would prove more important than any other **factor** in attracting customers. Walmart's **incredibly sophisticated** distribution, **inventory**, and **scanner** systems meant that customers almost never **encountered depleted** shelves or price-check delays.

Meanwhile, Kmart's mounted, as distribution horror stories **abounded**. Employees lacked the training and skills to plan and control inventory properly, and Kmart's cash registers often did not have **up-to-date information** and would scan items and enter incorrect prices. This led to a **lawsuit** in California, and Kmart settled for US $985,000 for **overcharging** its customers.

Over the years, it has been Walmart's focus on logistical matters that enables it to keep its prices low, its customer happy and returning often. Today, Walmart is nearly six times the size of Kmart.

Kmart continued its focus on ad **circulars** and promotional pricing into the 21st century, whereas Walmart continued to focus more on supply chain efficiency and less on advertising with the result that selling, administrative, and **overhead** costs were 17.3 percent for Walmart and Kmart's were 22.7 percent. Walmart was able to achieve prices that average 3.8 percent below Kmart's and even 3.2 percent below Target's. In 2002, Kmart went into **bankruptcy** and **reorganization**.

【Outline】

Logistics management is a **fundamental** concept that has evolved to enable organizations to improve their efficiency and effectiveness in the 21st century. We start our study of logistics management by discussing the meaning of logistics management and important management activities in the logistics functions. Then we discuss the visibility of logistic system.

【Key Words】

retail ['ri:teil]	n.	零售业
	vt.	零售，零卖；转述；传播
merchandise chains		商业连锁店
dotted ['dɔtid]	adj.	星罗棋布的；有点的
metropolitan [ˌmetrə'pɔlitən]	adj.	大城市的，都市的
rural ['ruərəl]	adj.	田园的，乡村的
consider [kən'sidə(r)]	v.	认为，考虑；顾及
mission ['miʃn]	n.	使命，任务
analyst ['ænəlist]	n.	分析者，分析师
attribute...to...		将……归结为……
primarily [prai'merəli]	adv.	首先；主要地，根本上
philosophy [fə'lɔsəfi]	n.	哲学，哲学思想；生活信条
urban ['ɜ:bən]	adj.	城市的，都市的
presence ['prezns]	n.	出席，到场；存在
visibility [ˌvizə'biləti]	n.	可见度，可见性；能见度，清晰度
stand-alone[①]	adj.	独立经营的
aging downtown		老城区
executive [ig'zekjətiv]	n.	主管人员，领导层
marketing ['mɑ:kitiŋ]	n.	市场营销；市场学
merchandise ['mɜ:tʃəndaiz]	n.	商品，货物
	vt.	买卖，销售
obsess [əb'ses]	vt.	时刻困扰；缠住，迷住
headquarters [ˌhed'kwɔ:təz]	n.	总部，总店

---

① 复合词是英语中的一类词汇，通常以"-"连接单词构成，或者以短语构成，一般有复合名词、复合形容词、复合动词等形式。

enable [iˈneibl]	vt.	使能够；使可行
restock [ˌriːˈstɔk]	v.	重新进货，再储存
distribution center		配送中心
enhance [inˈhɑːns]	v.	提高，增强；改进
cultivate [ˈkʌltiveit]	v.	培养；耕作，种植；结交
loyalty [ˈlɔiəlti]	n.	忠诚，忠心
factor [ˈfæktə(r)]	n.	因素，要素
incredible [inˈkredəbl]	adj.	难以置信的，不可思议的；惊人的
sophisticated [səˈfistikeitid]	adj.	复杂的；富有经验的；精密的，尖端的（sophisticate 的过去分词）
inventory [ˈinvəntri]	n.	详细目录；存货清单，存货总值
scanner [ˈskænə(r)]	n.	扫描器，扫描仪；检测装置
encounter [inˈkauntə(r)]	vt.	遇到，遭遇；偶遇，邂逅
	n.	偶遇
deplete [diˈpliːt]	vt.	使大量减少；消耗
abound [əˈbaund]	vi.	大量存在；充满，丰富
up-to-date information		最新信息
lawsuit [ˈlɔːsuːt]	n.	诉讼
overcharge [ˌəuvəˈtʃɑːdʒ]	vt.	要价过高
circular [ˈsɜːkjələ(r)]	adj.	圆形的，环形的；循环的
overhead [ˌəuvəˈhed]	adj.	上面的；经常的；管理的
	n.	经常性支出，运营费用
bankruptcy [ˈbæŋkrʌptsi]	n.	破产
reorganization [riːˌɔːgənaiˈzeiʃən]	n.	组建，改编；重组；整顿

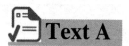

What Is Logistics?

After completing a **commercial transaction**, logistics will execute the transfer of goods from the supplier (seller) to the customer (buyer) in the most cost-effective manner.[1] This is the **definition** of logistics management. During the transfer process, **hardware** such as logistics facilities and equipment (logistics carriers) are needed, as well as information control and standardization. In addition, supports from the government and logistics association should be in place.

Logistics is a **unique** global "pipeline" that operates 24 hours a day,[2] seven days a week and 52 weeks a year, planning and **coordinating** the **transport** and **delivery** of products and service to customers all over the world. **Coming into being** with the advent of civilization, logistics is anything but a **newborn** baby.[3] However, when it comes to modern logistics, most **professionals** in the business consider it one of the most **challenging** and exciting jobs, **invisible** as it is.[4]

Chapter 1 Logistics Management

Modern logistics is related to the **effective** and **efficient** flow of materials and information. They are of **vital** importance to customers and **clients** in various sections of the economic society which may include but by no means is limited to: **packaging**, **warehousing**, material handling, inventory, transport, **forecasting**, strategic planning, and customer service.

"Logistics is that part of the supply chain process that plans, implements and controls the efficient, effective flow and storage of goods, service and related information from the point of origin to the point of consumption to meet customers' requirements." Although this definition fails to incorporate all specific terms used in the study of logistics, it does reflect the need for total movement management from point of material procurement to location of finished product distribution.

―――――――――― ••••• ――――――――――

【 Key Words 】

commercial [kəˈmɜːʃl]	adj.	商业的，贸易的
transaction [trænˈzækʃn]	n.	交易；办理，处理
definition [ˌdefiˈnɪʃn]	n.	定义，解说
hardware [ˈhɑːdweə(r)]	n.	五金器具；硬件，部件
unique [juˈniːk]	adj.	唯一的；独特的
pipeline [ˈpaɪplaɪn]	n.	管道；输送管线
coordinate [kəʊˈɔːdɪneɪt]	vt.	调整，整合；协调，搭配
transport [ˈtrænspɔːt]	n.	运输，运输工具
	vt.	传送，运输；流放，放逐
delivery [dɪˈlɪvəri]	n.	递送；交付，交货
come into being		形成，产生
newborn [ˈnjuːbɔːn]	adj.	新生的，初生的

professional [prəˈfeʃənl]	n.	专业人员
	adj.	专业的，职业的
challenging [ˈtʃælindʒiŋ]	adj.	富有挑战性的；艰巨的
invisible [inˈvizəbl]	adj.	看不见的，无形的
effective [iˈfektiv]	adj.	有效的，起作用的
efficient [iˈfiʃnt]	adj.	效率高的，有能力的
vital [ˈvaitl]	adj.	重大的，必要的
client [ˈklaiənt]	n.	顾客，客户；委托人
package [ˈpækidʒ]	n.	包裹；包装，包装盒
warehouse [ˈweəhaus]	n.	仓库
forecast [ˈfɔːkɑːst]	vt.	预测

【Notes to Text A】

[1] After completing a commercial transaction, logistics will execute the transfer of goods from the supplier (seller) to the customer (buyer) in the most cost-effective manner.

"after completing a commercial transaction" 是以"介词＋动词＋ing"引导的时间状语。

[2] Logistics is a unique global "pipeline" that operates 24 hours a day.

这句话所用的修辞手法是比喻。比喻分为两类：明喻和暗喻。明喻称被比喻的物体"像某个事物"，用"like"表示；暗喻称某个事物"是另一个事物"，用"is"表示。例如："Jack looks like a wonder boy" 是明喻；"Jack is a wonder" 是暗喻。

[3] Coming into being with the advent of civilization, logistics is anything but a new-born baby.

"coming into being with…" 意为"一直以来就和……一起"。

"anything but" 意为"并非，不是"，"nothing but" 意为"就是，正是"，要注意两者的区别。

[4] However, when it comes to modern logistics, most professionals in the business consider it one of the most challenging and exciting jobs, invisible as it is.

"invisible as it is" 是一个倒装句句式，表示"尽管……"，"as" 前面可加名词或形容词。例如：

Child as he is, he makes a living on his own. 尽管他还是小孩，但已经自己谋生了。

Difficult as it is, we still encourage each other. 尽管很困难，但我们仍然互相鼓励。

【Exercises to Text A】

I. Fill in the blanks.

1. Logistics is a unique global "_____" that operates 24 hours a day; 7 days a week and 52 weeks a year.

2. Coming into being with the advent of civilization, logistics is anything but a _____ baby.

3. Logistics is that part of _____ process that plans, implements and controls the efficient, effective flow and storage of goods, service and related information from the point of origin to the point of consumption to meet customers' requirements.

II. True or false.

1. When it comes to modem logistics, most professionals in the business consider it one of the worst jobs.

(   )

2. Modern logistics is related to the effective and efficient flow of materials and information. (   )

3. Modern logistics may include only: packaging, warehousing, material handling, inventory, transport, forecasting, strategic planning, and customer service. (   )

III. Translation.

1. During the transfer process, hardware such as logistics facilities and equipment (logistics carriers) are needed, as well as information control and standardization. In addition, supports from the government and logistics association should be in place.

2. Logistics is a unique global "pipeline" that operates 24 hours a day; seven days a week and 52 weeks a year, planning and coordinating the transport and delivery of products and service to customers all over the world.

3. Modern logistics is related to the effective and efficient flow of materials and information are of vital importance to customers and clients in various sections of the economic society which may include but by no means is limited to: packaging, warehousing, material handling, inventory, transport, forecasting, strategic planning, and customer service.

4. Logistics is that part of the supply chain process that plans, implements and controls the efficient, effective flow and storage of goods, service and related information from the point of origin to the point of consumption to meet customers' requirements.

**Text B**

Develop Systems Visibility to Material Shipment

Up-to-the-minute information **concerning** the status and location of **shipments** can provide at least partial visibility that is required for total material control.[1] The need for control supports the development of electronic data and **communications systems** between **carrier** and buyer. <u>Third party logistics</u>[①] companies (3PLs) should be able to provide **immediate access to information** on shipment status, whether on motor carriers linked electronically with shippers through **global positioning systems** or on a ship, aircraft, or customs' location. [2]

Many 3PLs offer detailed shipment **tracking systems** to provide current status updates. Several levels of **complexity** exist in these systems. One-way information systems allow a buyer to gain information about the location of a shipment on a real time basis. A buyer simply requests data directly from a carrier's information system now often provided via the carrier's **website**.

However, many 3PLs now **utilize event-based systems**. These provide status **alerts** via e-mail, fax, pager, and so on, to a buyer or salesperson that a particular shipment has been delayed and that this may affect other entities in the supply chain (e.g., manufacturing plants, warehouse locations, and customers). Even though **problematic** events cannot always be prevented, early warning signals, using an event-management system, can help sourcing companies deal with the problem in a more timely manner. <u>This allows a buyer to realize improved service and greater benefits that otherwise might not be available through a traditional, **arm's length business relationship**.</u>[3] For example, a buyer may receive a **guarantee** that carrier equipment will be available when and where needed. Controlling and managing the movement of goods is easier and more efficient when a buyer selects only the best 3PLs available and develops a closer working relationship with them.

---

① third party logistics 第三方物流（一般缩写为 3PL） 根据《中华人民共和国国家标准　物流术语》（GB/T 18354—2021），第三方物流是指由独立于物流服务供需双方之外且以物流服务为主营业务的组织提供物流服务的模式。

Chapter 1 Logistics Management

【Key Words】

up-to-the-minute	adj.	最新的，最近的；直到现在的
concerning [kən'sɜ:nɪŋ]	prep.	关于，就……而言；与……相关（concern 的现在分词）
shipment [ʃɪp'mənt]	n.	装运；载货量；装货
communication system		通信系统，信息系统
carrier ['kærɪə(r)]	n.	承运人，载体；运送者，运输公司
immediate [ɪ'mi:dɪət]	adj.	即刻的；直接的；接近的
access to information		信息获取
global positioning system		全球定位系统（简称 GPS）
tracking system		跟踪系统，追踪系统
complexity [kəm'pleksəti]	n.	复杂性；难懂，难题
website ['websaɪt]	n.	网站
utilize ['ju:təlaɪz]	vt.	利用，使用
event-based system		事故预警系统
alert [ə'lɜ:t]	v.	通知，使……警觉
	n.	警报，警戒状态；通告
problematic [ˌprɒblə'mætɪk]	adj.	成问题的，有疑问的；不确定的
arm's length		公平的；保持距离；一般交易关系
guarantee [ˌgærən'ti:]	n.	保证，担保；保证人，保证书
	vt.	保证，担保

【Notes to Text B】

[1] Up-to-the-minute information concerning the status and location of shipments can provide at least partial visibility that is required for total material control.

"up-to-the-minute" 意为 "目前为止的"，这种结构为复合词。

[2] Third-party logistics companies（3PLs）should be able to provide immediate access to information on shipment status, whether on motor carriers linked electronically with shippers through global positioning systems or on a ship, aircraft, or customs' location.

"whether on motor carriers linked electronically with shippers through global positioning systems or on a ship, aircraft, or customs' location" 是 "whether" 引导的状语从句。

[3] This allows a buyer to realize improved service and greater benefits that otherwise might not be available through a traditional, arm's length business relationship.

"arm's length business relationship" 意为 "公平交易关系"；而 "Arm's Length Principle" 意为 "公平交易原则"。

【Exercises to Text B】

I. Fill in the blanks.

1. Up-to-the-minute information _____ the status and location of _____ can provide at least partial _____ that is required for total material control.

2. Third-party logistics companies should be able to provide _____ to information on shipment status, whether on motor carriers linked electronically with shippers through _____ or on a ship, aircraft, or customs' location.

3. Many 3PLs offer detailed shipment _____ systems to provide current status updates.

4. A buyer simply requests data directly from a carrier's information system now often provided via the carrier's _____.

5. However, many 3PLs now _____ event-based systems. These provide status _____ via e-mail, fax, pager, and so on, to a buyer or salesperson that a particular shipment has been delayed and that this may affect other entities in the supply chain (e.g., manufacturing plants, warehouse locations, and customers).

6. This allows a buyer to realize improved service and greater benefits that otherwise might not be available through a traditional, _____ business relationship.

II. Translation.

1. 物流货物可掌控的要求支持了承运商和客户之间电子数据和通信系统的发展。

2. 这些系统存在不同程度的复杂性。

3. 即使问题事件不能完全制止，使用事件预警系统提供早期预警信息能够帮助公司及早进入问题应对状态。

4. 单向信息系统允许买方获得实时的运输地点信息。

5. 买方可以获得承运方随时随地设备待命的保证。

Reading Material A

P.G. Logistics[①]

PGL provides total solutions as logistics and supply chain. PGL provides customers with optimized logistics network design, planning, operations, management and information related to supply chain management.

PGL has established more than 40 subsidiaries or branch offices in main cities across the nation, forming a service network that supports nationwide distribution. In addition, there are PGL offices in China, Thailand and Australia to develop international business. In 1997, PGL was the first logistics company that applied Internet/Intranet system to logistics information for servicing customers.

"Creating value for our customers" is the core operating principle of PGL. There are various professional **talents** who fully understand Chinese situation and western advanced management. PGL implements new technology, effective information systems and management practices in daily work, and continually improves operation **reliability** and customer satisfaction through a set of standards and procedures. As a result, PGL is recognized by its customers as one of best logistics suppliers in China. And some of customers formed a strategic **partnership** with PGL in a long run.

Recently, PGL is to build up about 10 distribution centers equipped with high efficient and advanced facilities and equipment, such as **RF**, **dock leveler**, **racking** and **WMS** etc.. The size of these distribution centers will be varied from 150,000 to 700,000 square meters. With completion of new distribution centers, PGL will have an effective and responsive distribution network across China to support, but not limited to the following:

(1) Warehousing and inventory management.

(2) Dispatching and transportation management.

(3) Distribution in cities.

(4) Order management.

(5) **Cross docking**.

(6) Value added service such as labeling, cutting, repackaging etc..

(7) Product shows.

---

① P. G. Logistics 宝供物流(缩写为PGL) 我国目前较具规模、影响力, 技术领先的第三方物流企业, 官网为 http://www.pgl-world.com/。

(8) Financial Transitions.

(9) Information providing and sharing.

(10) Customs Clearance and inspections related to import and export.

(11) Logistics research and development, training service.

All in all, PGL will provide **integrated** total supply chain solutions to customers both at home and abroad for them to grow their business.

【Key Words】

talent ['tælənt]	n.	人才；才能，天赋
reliability [ri‚laiə'biliti]	n.	可靠性，可靠度；可信赖
partnership ['pɑːtnəʃip]	n.	伙伴关系；合伙企业；合作关系
RF		Radio Frequency 的缩写，即无线射频
dock leveler		装卸跳板
racking ['rækiŋ]	v.	使痛苦，使焦虑
	adj.	拷问的；折磨人的
WMS		Warehouse Management System 的缩写，即仓库管理系统
cross docking		越库；直接换装；交叉配送；交叉转运
integrated ['intigreitid]	adj.	综合的；完整的，整体的
	v.	整合（integrate 的过去分词）

【Questions】

1. Discuss the functions of the logistics.
2. Give some examples to illustrate the importance of a firm's logistical activities.

Reading Material B

GM[①] Develops Vector as Its Fourth Party Logistics[②] Provider

To deal with increased complexity in a **build-to-order** environment, GM **sought** a 4PL

---

① GM 通用汽车公司（全拼是 General Motors） 美国汽车制造公司，总部设在美国底特律文艺复兴中心，其核心汽车业务及子公司遍布全球。

② fourth party logistics 第四方物流（缩写为 4PL） 第四方物流为物流业者提供一个整合性的物流，是专门为第一方物流、第二方物流和第三方物流提供物流规划、咨询、物流信息系统和供应链管理等的活动。

partner within the logistics industry for the following reasons:

(1) Avoid/defer structural or **fixed costs**, and drive more costs to variable.

(2) Gain access to specialized logistics resources.

(3) Rapidly develop and **deploy cutting-edge** IT logistics solutions.

(4) Provide a single point of organizational **accountability** responsible for managing logistics activities.

A 4PL is a **distinctive** business model that extends outsourcing to new levels as it combines the best **capabilities** and technologies from logistics companies and other service organizations to deliver value through total supply chain management. Selecting a non-asset-based provider that is **neutral** with respect to selecting logistics shippers and materials management providers is a must.

GM's supply chains **were integrated with** logistics processes and IT management controlled by a 4PL, **leveraging** multiple service providers. Why was it important for GM to go with a 4PL? To reduce the cost of GM's huge logistics network, which includes raw materials providers (such as steel), customs brokers, 3PL providers, first and second-tier component suppliers, freight forwarders, **assembly** operations, original equipment manufacturers, distribution centers, new vehicle dealers, parts and service dealers, and 3PL distributors of aftermarket parts. Looking at this **hugely** complex network, GM's logistics team realized that nobody can do it all and that GM wasn't capable of managing this network themselves either. To cope with this complexity, GM signed a contract with CNF to form a 4PL **joint venture** called Vector SCM.

GM will be able to do the following:

(1) Retain strategic planning, benchmark, and operational **competency**.

(2) Have **board representation** and **super-majority** rights on critical issues.

(3) Reduce logistics costs through a gain share agreement.

(4) Avoid **significant** IT development costs.

(5) Provide full accountability to GM Global Logistics for all aspects of logistics Performance.

Vector will do the following:

(1) Manage GM's current global network of logistics service providers.

(2) Manage GM's global tactical and operational logistics activities.

(3) Enable logistics capabilities (visibility, speed, flexibility, and reliability).

(4) Provide **best-of-breed** logistics technology.

(5) Provide people, process, and technology to support GM global logistics operations.

(6) Part with leaders in the industry to build, buy, or leverage skills and technology.

GM and Vector SCM have created common global solutions across logistics networks through the use of regional Logistics Control Centers. Vector assumed the responsibility of managing approximately one third of GM's logistics spend. The gradual transition of responsibility to Vector SCM is well under way, managed through a disciplined business case process, involving discovery of opportunities, business case development, implementation, and business case approval. This has required major changes in the way that GM works and allows it to focus on its core competency of designing and building value for the end customer in the form of new vehicles and services.

【Key Words】

build-to-order	n.	按单生产，定制生产
sought [sɔːt]	v.	寻找（seek 的过去分词）
fixed cost		固定成本
deploy [diˈplɔi]	vt.	部署，调集；有效利用
cutting-edge	adj.	先进的，前沿的
accountability [əˌkaʊntəˈbiləti]	n.	义务；责任
distinctive [diˈstiŋktiv]	adj.	有特色的，与众不同的
capabilities [ˌkeipəˈbilətis]	n.	能力（capability 的复数形式）；功能，性能
neutral [ˈnjuːtrəl]	adj.	中立的，中性的；中立国的
	n.	中立国；中立人士
be integrated with		使与……结合
leveraging [ˈliːvəridʒiŋ]	n.	杠杆作用；举债经营
	v.	促使改变（leverage 的现在分词）
assembly [əˈsembli]	n.	装配；集会，集合；议会
hugely [ˈhjuːdʒli]	adv.	非常
joint venture		合资企业
competency [ˈkɔmpitənsi]	n.	能力；资格
board representation		董事会代表
super-majority	n.	多数
significant [sigˈnifikənt]	adj.	重要的；显著的；有意义的
	n.	象征
best-of-breed	n.	单项优势；最佳组合

【Questions】

1. What is the fourth-party logistics provider?
2. What is the difference between 3PL and 4PL?

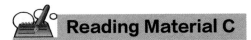 **Reading Material C**

Cold Chain Introduction

Cold chain management includes all of the means used to ensure a constant temperature (between +2℃ and+8℃) for a product that is not heat stable (such as **vaccines**, **serums**, tests, etc.), from the time it is manufactured until the time it is used.

The cold chain must never be broken. Vaccines are sensitive to heat and extreme cold and must be kept at the correct temperature at all times.

Health workers at all levels are often responsible for maintaining the cold chain while vaccines are stored in the vaccine stores at the province and county levels, or while they are being transported to township and villages, and while they are being used during **immunization** sessions or rounds. More and more often it is becoming the **logistician**'s responsibility to manage the cold chain as a part of the supply chain.

The logistics staff must be trained to both use and manage these materials. This includes having appropriate and efficient logistics mechanisms to manage shipping, fuel, spare parts etc.. Without training, the program will be seriously **compromised** and put at risk.

【Key Words】

vaccine [væk'si:n]	n.	疫苗；菌苗
	adj.	疫苗的；菌苗的
serum ['sirəm]	n	血清，免疫血清；浆液，精华液
immunization [ˌimjunə'zeiʃn]	n.	免疫
logistician [ˌləudʒi'stiʃən]	n.	物流师；军需官；后勤人员
compromise ['kɑːmprəmaiz]	n.	妥协；和解
	v.	妥协，折中；违背

【Questions】

1. What is the definition of cold chain management?
2. How to protect the goods in the cold supply chain from the coronavirus? (brainstorming)

Chapter 2
Supply Chain Management

Beer Game and Bullwhip Effect[1]

【参考音频】

The Beer Game was originally invented by Jay Forrester at MIT[2] Sloan School of

---

① Bullwhip Effect 牛鞭效应 牛鞭效应是经济学中的一个术语，供应链管理的基本原理之一，指的是供应链上的一种需求变异放大现象，是信息流从最终客户端向原始供应商端传递时，无法有效地实现信息的共享，使得信息扭曲而逐级放大，导致需求信息出现越来越大的波动，此信息扭曲的放大作用在图形上很像一根甩起的牛鞭，因此被形象地称为牛鞭效应。可以将处于上游的供应商比作梢部，下游的客户比作根部，一旦根部抖动，传递到末梢端就会出现很大的波动。

② MIT 麻省理工学院（Massachusetts Institute of Technology） 世界上最杰出的理工大学之一。

Management[①] in early 1960's. It is a simulation game that can be used to **demonstrate** the benefits of information sharing, **e-collaboration** in the supply chain and a number of key principles of supply chain management.

Before a game begins, something about the game must be known:

1. Roles

(1) There are four roles in the game: retailer, **wholesaler**, distributor and manufacturer. See Figure 2.1.

(2) Each role from different company is each other's customer or supplier in a supply chain.

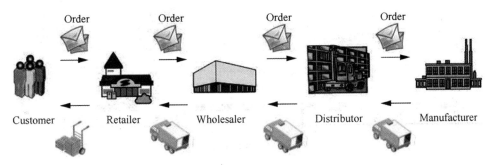

Figure 2.1 Roles in the game

2. Ground Rules

(1) A game extends over a **fictitious** year and covers 52 rounds of one week each. You cannot take a break in the entire game.

(2) For the sake of **simplicity**, everyone sells only one product: Lover's Beer. One unit = One crate of beer.

(3) There are three costs involved in the game: inventory carrying costs=US $1/case/week; the **backlog** costs=US $2/case/week; total cost = sum of costs at all four stages.

(4) Goal is Minimizing Total Supply Chain Cost! You need to do all the calculations, and decide how much you will order each week.

(5) It takes two weeks for replenishment order to reach; shipment time is also two weeks.

(6) All demand is to be satisfied! If for some reason you cannot deliver, the product is noted as backlog and you must deliver this order next time you have products in stock.

(7) NO COMMUNICATION BETWEEN STAGES! Retailers must not reveal actual customer orders!

(8) Players must not exchange any information other than that constituted by the order itself.

---

① MIT Sloan School of Management 麻省理工学院斯隆商学院 前身是麻省理工学院1895年班的Alfred P. Sloan（当时为通用汽车总裁）于1952年捐助500万美元成立的产业管理学院（School of Industrial Management）。1964年，该学院改名为斯隆管理学院（Alfred P. Sloan School of Management），以感谢赞助者。斯隆商学院被认为是美国最杰出的商学院之一，在2005年被《美国新闻与世界报道》杂志评选为美国排名第四的商学院，仅次于哈佛商学院、斯坦福大学商学院和宾夕法尼亚大学沃顿商学院。

3. Course of the Game

In each round, the following happens (see Figure 2.2):

(1) You receive goods from the supplier.

(2) You receive orders from the customer.

(3) You deliver to the customer as ordered.

(4) You order new goods.

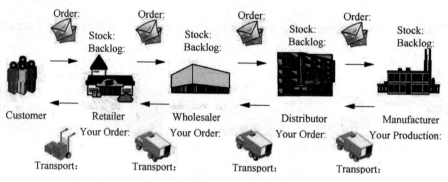

Figure 2.2 Course of the game

4. Figures and Diagrams (see Figure 2.3)

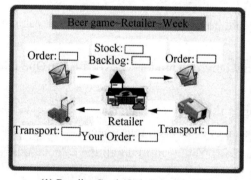

(1) Retailer Card (Only Retailer Use)

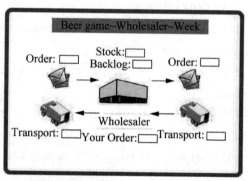

(2) Wholesaler Card (Only Wholesaler Use)

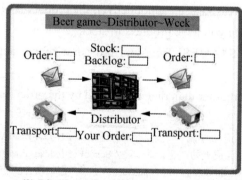

(3) Distributor Card (Only Distributor Use)

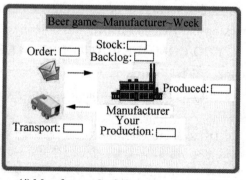

(4) Manufacturer Card (Only Manufacturer Use)

Figure 2.3 Figures and diagrams

Chapter 2 Supply Chain Management

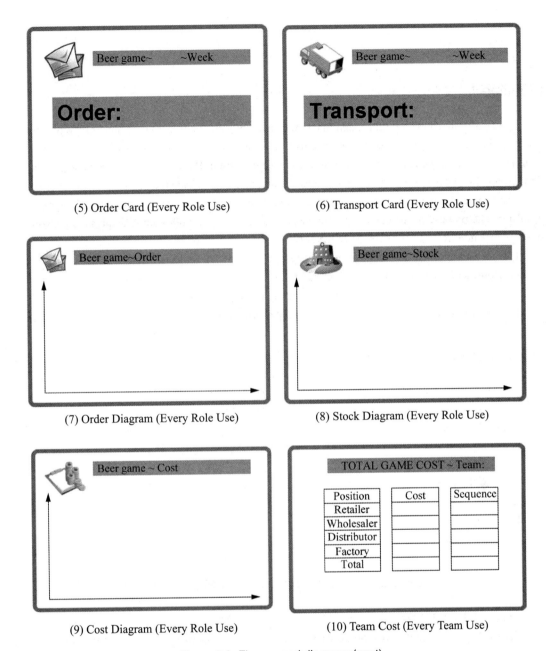

Figure 2.3 Figures and diagrams(next)

5. Start the Game

(1) Several games can take place at once, and several teams can therefore play against each other at the same time.

(2) Teacher plays the leader role in the game, to order 4 cases each week to the retailer in the first 4 weeks. From 4th week on, the leader can order any quantity.

(3) The game will last 50 weeks, but can be concluded at any time before that by the game leader. Now, the game leader starts the Game!

【Outline】

The results are shown in figures and diagrams when the game is over. Maybe most of the players feel frustrated because you are not getting the results you want. Feelings of confusion and disappointment are common. In the beer game players enact a four stage supply chain. Because communication and collaboration are not allowed between supply chain stages, players invariably create the so called bullwhip effect.

The beer game is a role-play supply chain simulation that lets us experience typical supply chain problems. The purpose of the game is to meet customer demand, through a multi-stage supply chain with minimal expenditure on back orders and inventory.

Prepare an analysis of the usage of the concepts you've learnt through the Beer Game.

(1) How can the performance be improved?
(2) What are the important factors affecting supply chain performance?
(3) How can IT help in improving supply chain performance?

【Key Words】

demonstrate ['demənstreit]	v.	证明；说明；（游行）示威；演示
e-collaboration	n.	电子协作
wholesaler ['həulseilə(r)]	n.	批发商
fictitious [fik'tiʃəs]	adj.	虚构的，编造的；假定的，虚设的，假装的
simplicity [sim'plisəti]	n.	简单，朴素；质朴，天真；无知
backlog ['bæklɔg]	n.	积压的事务；没交付的订货；存货，储备

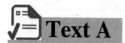 Text A

Introduction to Supply Chain Management

Supply Chain Management (SCM) is the management of the flow of goods and services. It includes the movement and storage of raw materials, work-in-process inventory, and finished goods from point of origin to point of consumption.[1] **Interconnected** or **interlinked** networks, channels and node businesses are involved in the **provision** of products and services required by end customers in a supply chain.[2]

Supply chain management has been defined as the "design, planning, **execution**, control, and **monitoring** of supply chain activities with the objective of creating net value, building a competitive **infrastructure**, **leveraging** worldwide logistics, **synchronizing** supply with demand and measuring performance globally".[3]

Chapter 2　Supply Chain Management

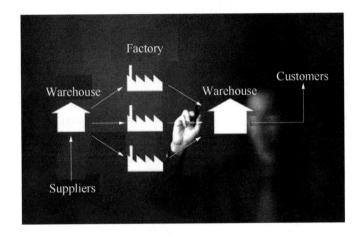

【参考视频】

A simple supply chain is made up of several elements that are linked by the movement of products along it.[4]

(1) Customer: The supply chain starts and ends with the customer. A customer starts the chain of events when he decides to purchase a product that has been offered for sale by a company. The customer contacts the sales department of the company, which enters the sales order for a specific **quantity** to be delivered on a specific date. If the product has to be manufactured, the sales order will include a requirement that needs to be fulfilled by the production **facility**.

(2) Planning: The requirement **triggered** by the customer's sales order will be **combined** with other orders. The planning department will create a production plan to produce the products to fulfill the customer's orders. To manufacture the products the company will then have to purchase the raw materials needed.

(3) Purchasing: The purchasing department receives a list of raw materials and services required by the production department to complete the customer's orders. The purchasing department sends purchase orders to selected suppliers to deliver the necessary raw materials to the manufacturing site on the required date.

(4) Inventory: The raw materials are received from the suppliers, checked for quality and **accuracy** and moved into the warehouse. The supplier will then send an invoice to the company for the items they delivered. The raw materials are stored until they are required by the production department.

(5) Production: Based on a production plan, the raw materials are moved inventory to the production area. The finished products ordered by the customer are manufactured using the raw materials purchased from suppliers. After the items have been completed and tested, they are stored back in the warehouse prior to delivery to the customer.

(6) Transportation: When the finished product arrives in the warehouse, the shipping department determines the most efficient method to ship the products so that they are delivered on or before the date specified by the customer. When the goods are received by the customer, the company will send an invoice for the delivered products.

【Key Words】

interconnected [ˌɪntəkəˈnɛkt]	adj.	连通的；相互连接的（interconnect 的过去分词）
interlinked [ɪntəˈlɪŋkt]	adj.	互连的（interlink 的过去分词）
provision [prəˈvɪʒn]	n.	供应；预备，准备；储备物资
execution [ˌeksɪˈkjuːʃn]	n.	履行，执行；实施，施行
monitoring [ˈmɒnɪtərɪŋ]	n.	监视，监控；检验，检查（monitor 的现在分词）
infrastructure [ˈɪnfrəstrʌktʃə(r)]	n.	基础建设，基础设施
leveraging [ˈliːvərɪdʒɪŋ]	n.	杠杆作用；优势；影响力，作用力（leverage 的现在分词）
synchronizing [ˈsɪŋkrənaɪzɪŋ]	adj.	同步的（synchronize 的现在分词）
quantity [ˈkwɒntəti]	n.	量，数量
facility [fəˈsɪləti]	n.	设施，设备；才能，天赋
triggered [ˈtrɪgəd]	v.	引发；发射（trigger 的过去分词）
	adj.	触发的
combined [kəmˈbaɪnd]	adj.	结合的；合并的（combine 的过去分词）
accuracy [ˈækjərəsi]	n.	准确（性），精确（性），精密（性）

【Notes to Text A】

[1] It includes the movement and storage of raw materials, work-in-process inventory, and finished goods from point of origin to point of consumption.

"work-in-process" 意为 "半成品"，其同义词有 "semi-finished goods" "half finished product"。

[2] Interconnected or interlinked networks, channels and node businesses are involved in the provision of products and services required by end customers in a supply chain.

be involved in 包括……中，被卷入……中；涉及……

be required by 被……要求。例如：be required by circumstances 势在必行

[3] Supply chain management has been defined as the "design, planning, execution, control, and monitoring of supply chain activities with the objective of creating net value, building a competitive infrastructure, leveraging worldwide logistics, synchronizing supply with demand and measuring performance globally".

with the objective of 以……为目标，在……目标下

[4] A simple supply chain is made up of several elements that are linked by the movement of products along it.

be made up of 由……所组成

【Exercises to Text A】

I. Fill in the blanks.

1. A simple supply chain is made up of several elements that are linked by the movement of products along it. It may include _____.

2. Design, planning, execution, control, and _____ of supply chain activities with the objective of creating net value, _____ a competitive infrastructure, _____ worldwide logistics, _____ supply with demand and measuring performance globally.

II. Translation.

1. 供应链以客户开始并以客户结束。

2. 当成品到达仓库，配送部门应制订运送产品的最有效的方案，以便能在指定的日期或之前交付客户。

 **Text B**

Top 8 Biggest Supply Chains

In recent years, companies the world over have invested heavily into **optimising** their supply chain processes in order to drive value across their operations.

1. Starbucks

Since opening its first store back in 1971, Starbucks has set out to be a "different kind of company". Its core mission is to inspire and **nurture** the human spirit-one person, one cup and one neighbourhood at a time. Starbucks currently has more than 24,000 stores across more than 75 markets. Since announcing a company-wide supply chain **reinvention** in 2008, Starbucks has continuously delivered on its promise. In 2018, the company announced a **commitment** to operate 10,000 "greener stores" by 2020.

2. PepsiCo

With brands such as Pepsi, Doritos, Mountain Dew and Quaker under its umbrella, Pepsi-Co is one of the largest food and beverage companies in the world. To this end,[1] it recognises the level of responsibility it has to ensure efficiency and best practice across its entire supply chain. In 2018, speaking at the Consumer Analyst Group of New York, PepsiCo detailed how it would use **automation** and data analytics to transform its supply chain and match the rising e-commerce landscape. In early 2019, the company collaborated with Robby Technologies to pilot a fleet of **autonomous** robots to deliver **snacks** and drinks to students at the University of the Pacific in California.

3. Nestle

The world's largest food and beverage company with more than 2,000 brands present in 189 countries, Nestle **incorporated** a number of global supply chain initiatives in 2018. In late 2018, the company announced an accelerated plan towards its 2020 No **Deforestation** commitment. This will involve becoming the first food company to implement a satellite-based service to monitor 100% of its global palm oil supply chain. "Our 'eyes in the sky' will monitor our palm oil supply chain 24/7, regardless of their certification status. This will enable us to further disclose publicly what we find, where we choose to **suspend** non-compliant suppliers, and where we choose to engage and improve the situation," said Benjamin Ware, Global Head of Responsible Sourcing, Nestlé S.A..

4. Intel

Tech behemoth Intel, based in Santa Clara, U.S.A., is a key player in the digital transformation of supply chains worldwide but in recent years, the company looked at its own supply chain and embraced this digital revolution. In 2017, the company embarked on a major digital transformation of its supply chain systems and implemented SAP HANHA to power this journey. Following a $208mn investment, Intel will simply its supply chain and data pipelines, enable self-service analysis to make smarter business decisions, improve the quality of supply chain data.

5. Colgate-Palmolive

Operating in more than 200 countries, Colgate-Palmolive is the premier manufacturer and distributor of consumer products including oral care, personal care and pet **nutrition** products. Much like Intel, Colgate also entered into a partnership with SAP to improve its supply chain analysis and to enable greater value for the business. The company is working towards SAP S/4HANA platform, which will free up time in other key areas of the business, explore new opportunities to drive growth and **utilise** SAP's cloud platform to collate this data and make smarter decisions.

6. Cisco Systems

Provider of industry-leading technology products and solutions, Cisco completely transformed its supply chain function in 2018 to boost agility, resiliency and ability to scale. Cisco identified that IT was "not able to respond quickly to supply chain business requirements, and the business was not able to respond quickly to market transitions and opportunities", said Shanthi Iyer, director, Cisco Value Chain IT, Supply Chain Management. Through the digital transformation, Cisco **migrated** all ERP instances into one, standardised, end-to-end system which resulted in a 30%～50% reduction in time to market.

7. Inditex

One of the world's largest fashion retailers, Spanish multinational company Inditex places sustainability at the heart of its supply chain operation. Challenging all of its 1,824 global suppliers to conform to a code of conduct as part of a **sustainability pledge**, Inditex was recognised in 2018 as the most sustainable retailer on the Dow Jones Sustainability Index.[2] Inditex was given some of the highest scores in the fashion sector in multiple categories, most notably Supply Chain Management.

8. Unilever

With a truly diversified portfolio ranging from foods, soaps, shampoos and everyday household products, Unilever is the world leader in consumer goods. In 2018, Unilever was recognised as a global leader for its actions and strategies which aim to manage carbon emissions and climate change across its supply chain. Assessed by non-profit environmental disclosure platform, CDP, Unilever was ranked amongst just 2% of 3,300 companies to be awarded a position on its leader board. As Unilever's Chief Supply Chain Officer, Marc Engel, said: "Disclosure through CDP helps us understand our upstream footprint better, what initiatives key suppliers have embarked on to reduce emissions associated with goods and services purchased, and to uncover opportunities for collaboration. Transparency and reporting are vital in building trust among consumers, customers, the communities we operate in, employees and also with our investors."

【Key Words】

optimising ['ɔptimaiziŋ]	vt.	使优化；充分利用
	vi.	表示乐观（optimise 的现在分词）
nurture ['nɜːtʃə(r)]	vt.	养育；鼓励；培植
	n.	养育；教养；营养物
reinvention [ˌriːin'venʃn]	n.	重塑；再造
commitment [kə'mitmənt]	n.	承诺，保证；委托；承担义务
automation [ˌɔːtə'meiʃn]	n.	自动化
autonomous [ɔ'tɔnəməs]	adj.	自治的；自主的
snack [snæk]	n.	点心，快餐；易办到的事
	v.	吃点心（快餐）
incorporated [in'kɔːpəreitid]	adj.	合并的；组成法人组织的
	v.	合并，包含；组成公司（incorporate 的过去分词）
deforestation [ˌdiːfɔːri'steiʃn]	n.	毁林；采伐森林，森林砍伐
suspend [sə'spend]	vt.	延缓，推迟；使暂停；使悬浮
nutrition [nju'triʃn]	n.	营养，营养学；营养品
utilise ['juːtilaiz]	vt.	使用，利用
migrate [mai'greit]	vi.	移动；随季节而移居；移往
	vt.	使移居；使移植

sustainability [sə,steinə'biləti] n. 持续性，永续性；能维持性
pledge [pledʒ] n. 保证，誓言；抵押，抵押品
  v. 保证，许诺；用……抵押

【Notes to Text B】

[1] to this end... 因为这个；为了这个（目的）
[2] Dow Jones Sustainability Index 道琼斯可持续发展指数

【Exercises to Text B】

Fill in the blanks.

Company	Chinese Name	Products
Starbucks		
PepsiCo		
Nestle		
Intel		
Colgate-Palmolive		
Cisco Systems		
Inditex		
Unilever		

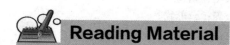

Reading Material

Blockchain Used to Track Cashmere Supply Chain

Canadian firm Convergence.tech used **blockchain** to help Mongolian farmers track and certify **cashmere** as part of efforts to create a sustainable supply chain.

Cashmere, which was once considered a luxury fibre, is now an affordable commodity. As a result, grasslands in Mongolia are rapidly degrading, while herders face income instability and are often indebted to intermediaries for cash advances.

"The social impact created by underpaid farmers and an opaque supply chain is also a source of concern. With alarm bells ringing worldwide, particularly in the fashion industry, we need to respond urgently," Convergence said.

A pilot project, launched in partnership with the United Nations Development Program, employed Convergence's **traceability** platform to test the creation of a sustainable and connected value chain. It involved 70 herders and eight cooperatives.

The firm developed a mobile app as part of the pilot to allow herders in Mongolia to easily register cashmere bales. Bales and packing slips were also attached to high-frequency RFID tags.

"This technology helped to mitigate risks by eradicating the traditional manual processes that were time-consuming and prone to human error," the tech firm said.

Around 471kg of cashmere was tracked across three provinces in northeastern Mongolia, from shearing at herders' homes to a processing facility in the Mongolian capital, Ulaanbaatar.

As well as benefiting the farmers, Convergence said the technology would allow buyers to identify the source of cashmere and help create a market that connects buyers interested in sustainability with sellers who follow sustainable practices.

Chami Akmeemana, CEO at Convergence.tech, said: "The nomadic community is one of immense pride but one with a volatile and unstable income. Leveraging blockchain technology within the transformation of the cashmere industry can provide numerous benefits for Mongolian herders, buyers, and sellers alike."

Mongolia produces 40% of cashmere globally, though the fibre accounts for less than 3.4% of its exports, which are dominated by mining. In 2018, the Mongolian government launched the National Cashmere Programme to improve its competitiveness.

【Key Words】

blockchain [blɔk'tʃein]　　　　　　n.　区块链
cashmere ['kæʃmiə(r)]　　　　　　n.　开司米，山羊绒；开司米羊毛织品
traceability [ˌtreisə'biləti]　　　　　n.　可描绘，可描写，可追溯；追源；可追踪性

【Questions】

1. What is "blockchain"?
2. Discuss about the advantages of blockchain.

Chapter 3
Transport Management

The Snakes and Ladders Game

【参考音频】

  The Snakes and **Ladders** Game is a classic **board game** which students can use a **dice** to move counters up ladders and down snakes. At the beginning, teacher may divide students into some groups and let each group play this game according to the game rules. The game aims to help students with recalling, **associating**, **distinguishing**, resolving, remembering information and knowledge of transportation facility and modes.

Chapter 3 Transport Management

 The Snakes and Ladders Game in Transportation Lesson

(Produced by Cong Qian, NJCC)

		Game Rules
	1	The game can be played by 4 or more players, simulate the process of passing an interview.
	2	Each player chooses a marker of a different color and places it on the START square.
	3	Each player rolls a dice and reads the number that he or she rolls.
	4	If a player lands on a question square, they must answer the question. Answers will be judged by other players to be a good idea (correct) or a bad idea (incorrect). If other members of the group disagree, the player must go back to the last square.
	5	If the player lands at the bottom of a ladder, he or she **climbs up**.
	6	If the player lands on a snake's head, he or she **slides down**.
	7	If the player lands on a surprise square, he or she chooses a card from the surprise pile and does as it says. If the player refuses to follow the instructions on the surprise card, he or she must lose a turn.
	8	The winner is the one who first reaches No.50.

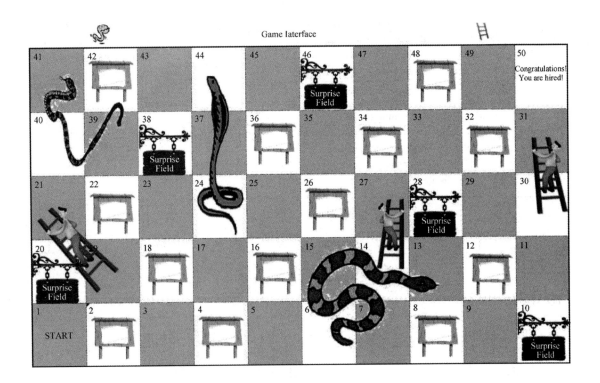

Game Ianterface

		Interview Questions	
Can you tell us what are the first forms of transport?	Which kind material was the first watercraft made of, wood or metal?	Interviewers want you to explain 2 examples of fixed installations, such as railway stations etc..	What's the difference between airport and aircraft?
Interviewers want you to list four kinds of vehicles, such as bus etc..	Can you tell us some modes of transportation, such as railway?	In your opinion, what's the differences between rail transport and road transport?	In your opinion, what's the differences between rail transport and water transport?
In your opinion, what's the differences between rail transport and air transport?	In your opinion, what's the differences between air transport and road transport?	In your opinion, what's the differences between water transport and road transport?	Have you ever heard of pipeline transport? Please give us an example.
Would you please tell us strengths and weaknesses of rail transport?	Would you please tell us strengths and weaknesses of air transport?	Would you please tell us strengths and weaknesses of water transport?	Would you please tell us strengths and weaknesses of road transport?
		Surprise Card	
Surprise Card Please move three steps forward for your excellent performance.	Surprise Card Please move two steps forward for your good performance.	Surprise Card Enter the last round of the interview, go to No.42.	Surprise Card Please move two steps back for your mistakes in the interview.
Surprise Card Failed to pass the written examination, please wait for next chance.	Surprise Card Please move three steps back for your mistakes in the interview.	Surprise Card	Surprise Card

【Key Words】

ladder ['lædə(r)]   n. 梯子，阶梯；途径；梯状物
board game   棋盘游戏
dice [dais]   n. 骰子
     v. 将……切成丁
associating [əˈsəuʃieitiŋ]   v. （使）结合，联合；（使）发生联系（associate 的现在分词）

Chapter 3　Transport Management

distinguishing [dɪsˈtɪŋgwɪʃɪŋ]	*adj.*	有区别的
	v.	辨别，区别（distinguish 的现在分词）；（使）出众；看清
climb up		向上爬；攀登
slide down		往下滑，滑下；塌陷

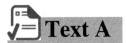Text A

History of Transport

　　Transport or transportation is the movement of people and goods from one location to another. Humans' first means of transport were walking and swimming.

　　The first forms of road transport were horses, **oxen** or even humans carrying goods over **dirt tracks** that often followed game trails.[1] **Paved** roads were first built by the Roman Empire, to allow armies to travel quickly. The first watercraft was canoes cut out from tree **trunks**. Early water transport was accomplished with ships that were either rowed or used the wind for **propulsion**, or a combination of the two. Until the **Industrial Revolution**, transport remained slow and costly.

【参考视频】

　　The Industrial Revolution in the 19th century saw a number of inventions fundamentally change transport. The invention of the steam engine, closely followed by its application in rail transport, made land transport independent of human or animal muscles.

　　The development of the combustion engine and the automobile at the turn into the 20th century, road transport became more **viable**, allowing the introduction of mechanical private transport.[2] The first highways were constructed during the 19th century with **macadam**. Later, **tarmac** and **concrete** became the **dominant** paving material. In 1903, the first controllable airplane was invented, and after World War Ⅰ, it became a fast way to transport people and express goods over long distances.

After World War Ⅱ, the automobile and airlines took higher shares of transport, reducing rail and water to freight and short-haul passenger. Spaceflight was launched in the 1950s, with rapid growth until the 1970s, when interest **dwindled**. In the 1950s, the introduction of containerization gave massive efficiency gains in freight transport, permitting globalization. International air travel became much more accessible in the 1960s, with the **commercialization** of the jet engine. Along with the growth in automobiles and motorways, this introduced a decline for rail and water transport. After the introduction of the Shinkansen in 1964, high-speed rail in Asia and Europe started taking passengers on long-haul routes from airlines.

【Key Words】

oxen ['ɔksən]	n.	牛，公牛（ox 的复数形式）
dirt track		泥铺道路
pave [peiv]	vt.	铺设；为……铺平道路；安排
trunk [trʌŋk]	n.	树干；大箱子；躯干
propulsion [prə'pʌlʃən]	n.	推进；推动力
Industrial Revolution		工业革命
viable ['vaiəbl]	adj.	切实可行的；有望实现的
macadam [mə'kædəm]	n.	铺路用的碎石料；柏油碎石路面
tarmac ['tɑːmæk]	vt.	以碎石和沥青铺盖（某物）表面
concrete ['kɔnkriːt]	n.	混凝土
	v.	用混凝土浇筑
	adj.	混凝土制的；具体的；实在的
dominant ['dɔminənt]	adj.	占支配地位的；显著的
dwindled ['dwindld]	vi.	逐渐变少或变小（dwindle 的过去分词）
commercialization [kə,mɜːʃəlai'zeiʃn]	n.	商业化，商品化

【Notes to Text A】

[1] The first forms of road transport were horses, oxen or even humans carrying goods over dirt tracks that often followed game trails.

"dirt tracks" 是 "dirt track" 的复数形式，意为 "泥铺道路"。

"game" 意为 "猎物的，野味的，野兽的；与狩猎有关的"。

[2] The development of the combustion engine and the automobile at the turn into the 20th century, road transport became more viable, allowing the introduction of mechanical private transport.

"turn into" 意为 "进入，走进"。

Chapter 3 Transport Management

【 Exercises to Text A 】

Fill in the blanks.

Period or Item	Example	Example
Humans' first means of transport		
The first forms of road transport		
The first watercraft		
The steam engine era		
The combustion engine era		

Text B

Transportation Elements

Transportation elements include **infrastructure**, **vehicles**, and operations.

1. Infrastructure

Infrastructure is the fixed installations that allow a vehicle to operate. It consists of the fixed installations necessary for transport, and may be roads, railways, airways, waterways, canals and pipelines, and **terminals** such as airports, railway stations, bus stations, warehouses, trucking terminals, **refueling depots** (including fueling docks and fuel stations), and seaports. [1]

Infrastructure consists of both a way, terminal and facilities for parking and maintenance. For rail, pipeline, road and cable transport, the entire way the vehicle travels must be built up. Aircraft and watercraft are able to avoid this, since the airway and seaway do not need to be built up. However, they require fixed infrastructure at terminals.

Terminals such as airports, ports and stations, are locations where passengers and freight can be transferred from one mode to another. For passenger transport, terminals are integrating different modes to allow riders to **interchange** to take advantage of each mode's advantages. For freight, terminals act as **transshipment** points, though some cargo is transported directly from the point of production to the point of use.

The financing of infrastructure can either be public or private. Transport is often a natural **monopoly** and a necessity for the public; roads, and in some countries railways and airports are funded through taxation. New infrastructure projects can involve large spending, and are often financed through debt.

2. Vehicle

A vehicle is any non-living device that is used to move people and goods. Unlike the infrastructure, the vehicle moves along with the cargo and riders. Vehicles may include automobiles, bicycles, buses, trains, trucks, people, **helicopters**, and aircraft.

Vehicles that do not operate on land, are usually called crafts. Unless being pulled by a cable or muscle-power, the vehicle must provide its own propulsion; this is most commonly done through a steam engine, **combustion** engine, electric motor, a jet engine or a rocket, though other means of propulsion also exist.[2] Vehicles also need a system of **converting** the energy into movement; this is most commonly done through wheels, **propellers** and pressure.

Vehicles are most commonly staffed by a driver. However, some systems, such as people movers and some rapid transits, are fully automated. For passenger transport, the vehicle must have a compartment for the passengers. Simple vehicles, such as automobiles, bicycles or simple aircraft, may have one of the passengers as a driver.

3. Operation

For public transport and freight transport, operations are done through private enterprise or by governments. The infrastructure and vehicles may be owned and operated by the same company, or they may be operated by different entities. Traditionally, many countries have had a national airline and national railway. Since the 1980s, many of these have been privatized. International shipping remains a highly competitive industry with little **regulation**, but ports can be public owned.

【Key Words】

infrastructure [ˈinfrəstrʌktʃə(r)]	n.	基础设施；基础建设
vehicle [ˈviːəkl]	n.	车辆，交通工具；手段，工具
terminal [ˈtɜːminl]	n.	终端；终点站；航空站；集散地
refueling depot		加油站
interchange [ˈintətʃeindʒ]	v.	交换，互换
	n.	交换，交替；互通式立体交叉，道路立体枢纽
transshipment [ˈtrænsʃipmənt]	n.	转运；转载
monopoly [məˈnɔpəli]	n.	垄断；专卖
helicopter [ˈhelikɔptə(r)]	n.	直升机
combustion [kəmˈbʌstʃən]	n.	燃烧；氧化
convert [kənˈvɜːt]	v.	（使）转变；换算；改变（信仰）；使……迷上
propeller [prəˈpelə(r)]	n.	螺旋桨，推进器
regulation [ˌregjuˈleiʃn]	n.	管理；控制；规章；规则
	adj.	规定的；必须使用的

【Notes to Text B】

[1] It consists of the fixed installations necessary for transport, and may be roads, railways, airways, waterways, canals and pipelines, and terminals such as airports, railway stations, bus stations, warehouses, trucking terminals, refueling depots (including fueling docks and fuel stations), and seaports.

  fixed installations　固定装置
  trucking terminals　卡车货运站

[2] Unless being pulled by a cable or muscle-power, the vehicle must provide its own propulsion; this is most commonly done through a steam engine, combustion engine, electric motor, a jet engine or a rocket, though other means of propulsion also exist.

  "muscle-power" 意为 "力量牵引"。
  "means of" 在本句中意为 "……的工具"，例如：
  The train is a safe means of transportation. 火车是一种安全可靠的交通工具。

【Exercises to Text B】

Fill in the blanks.

Infrastructure	Vehicle	
Airport		Helicopter
	Bullet Train	Train
	Barge	
	Bus	Truck

Text C

Transportation Mode

Transport is performed by modes, such as rail, road, water, air, pipeline, **cable** and space. Each mode has its advantages and disadvantages, and will be chosen for a trip on the basis of cost, capability, route and speed.

In this text, we will look at five modes separately, emphasizing the factors which give one mode advantages over others, or which put that mode at a disadvantage.

Chapter 3 Transport Management

1. Rail Transport

Rail transport is where a train runs along a set of two **parallel** steel rails, known as a railway or railroad. The **locomotive** can be powered by steam, diesel or by electricity supplied by **trackside** systems. Rail network is used for moving large volumes of freight over long distances. Regional and **commuter** trains feed cities from suburbs and surrounding areas, while intra-urban transport is performed by high-capacity tramways and rapid **transits**, often making up the backbone of a city's public transport.[1] Freight trains traditionally used box cars, requiring **manual** loading and unloading of the cargo.

Strengths:

(1) Rail transport offers cost advantages for high volume or long distance hauls.

(2) High average speeds for journeys in the arrange of 50 to 300 miles, which is especially important for passengers.

(3) The safety record of the railway is excellent with both passengers and freight. This is especially true with the carriage of hazardous cargo.

(4) Of all the land-based modes, the railways are least affected by bad weather.

Weaknesses:

One of the major weaknesses of railway is the inherent inflexibility of operation, fixed (non-flexible) time schedules and service from terminal to terminal rather than from stocking location to stocking location. It is almost impossible for the railways to adapt their infrastructure to meet the challenges of the changing patterns of economic and social activities.

2. Road Transport

A road is an **identifiable** route, way or path between two or more places. The most common road vehicle is the automobile; a wheeled passenger vehicle that carries its own motor. Other users of roads include buses, trucks, motorcycles, bicycles and **pedestrians**.

Strengths:

(1) The advantages of motor transport are flexibility of location, time and speed of delivery.

(2) Buses allow for more efficient travel at the cost of reduced flexibility.

(3) Road transport by truck is often the initial and final stage of freight transport.

Weaknesses:

(1) The size of the load is restricted by legislation with limits on vehicle size and weights, not by the prevailing technology and economies as with other modes.

(2) Roads are not used exclusively by one form of transport and **congestion** can occur which interferes with schedule planning and time keeping.

(3) Automobiles are deemed with high energy and area use, and the main source of noise and air pollution in cities.

3. Water Transport

Water transport is the process of transport a watercraft, such as a barge, boat, ship or sailboat, makes over a body of water, such as a sea, ocean, lake, canal or river. [2] Water transport is utilized for large loads of low-value-per-unit goods. In the 1800s, the first steam ships were developed, using a steam engine to drive a **paddle** wheel or propeller to move the ship. The steam was produced using wood or coal. Now most ships have an engine using a slightly refined type of petroleum called bunker fuel. Some specialized ships, such as **submarines**, use nuclear power to produce the steam.

Strengths:

(1) Modern sea transport is a highly effective method of transporting large quantities of **non-perishable** goods.

(2) For the users, this is the cheapest method of moving goods worldwide. Transport by water is significantly less costly than air transport for trans-continental shipping.

Weaknesses:

(1) The main **drawback** is the speed of the ship which is very slow especially when it is realized that the ship operates continuously without a break.

(2) Although ships are relatively safe, accidents can involve severe pollution and sometimes loss of life.

4. Air Transport

The aircraft is the second fastest method of transport, after the rocket. During the flight, the crew of an aircraft has to communicate with stations on the ground to give details of the position, receive information and instructions as to the position of other aircraft.

Strengths:

(1) The major strength of air transport is the speed of travel. The longer the distance of the flight, the greater the time saving of the customer.

(2) Short distances or in inaccessible places helicopters can be used.

(3) Air transport has a good public image and is perceived to be very **glamorous**.

Weaknesses:

(1) Inflexible in that an airplane has to land and take off at an airport, which is sited far away from the city centers.

(2) For freight, in comparison to sea transport, air transport is expensive for the shipper and the cargo carrying capacity is small. [3]

(3) High costs and energy use.

(4) The weather conditions is very important.

5. Pipeline Transport

Pipeline transport sends goods through a pipe; most commonly liquid and gases are sent. Any chemically stable liquid or gas can be sent through a pipeline. Short-distance systems exist for **sewage**, slurry, water and beer, while long-distance networks are used for **petroleum** and natural gas. [4]

Strengths:

(1) Pipelines are in the main environmentally sound as they can easily be buried, can traverse difficult **topography** and laid under water. They do not give off **fumes** or make a lot of noises, and can be **disguised** against visual **intrusion**.

(2) Another advantage is that they are largely automated with very few personnel needed to control the pumps and valves or to undertake maintenance.

Weaknesses:

(1) Costs of transport rise rapidly per unit handled as actual usage falls from the optimum because of the high proportion of fixed cost in the total cost of operation.

(2) They are inflexible geographically in that they are designed to serve fixed locations and there is a finite capacity which cannot be altered to accommodate sudden surges in demand.

【Key Words】

cable ['keibl]	n.	缆绳，钢索；电缆
parallel ['pærəlel]	adj.	平行的；类似的，相同的
	n.	平行线（面）；相似物；类比
locomotive [ˌləukə'məutiv]	n.	火车头，机车
	adj.	移动的；运动的
trackside ['træksaid]	n.	轨道旁，线路旁
commuter [kə'mju:tə(r)]	n.	（远距离）上下班往返的人
transit ['trænzit]	n.	运输，运送；经过，中转；交通运输系统
	adj.	中转的；过境的；临时的
manual ['mænjuəl]	adj.	用手的；手工的
	n.	使用手册；说明书
identifiable [aiˌdenti'faiəbl]	adj.	可辨认的
pedestrian [pə'destriən]	n.	步行者
congestion [kən'dʒestʃən]	n.	拥挤，堵车；充血；阻塞
paddle ['pædl]	n.	桨；桨状物
	vi.	用桨划动；涉水
submarine [ˌsʌbmə'ri:n]	n.	潜艇
non-perishable	adj.	不易损坏的；不易腐烂的
drawback ['drɔ:bæk]	n.	缺点，不利条件
glamorous ['glæmərəs]	adj.	富有魅力的；迷人的；独特的
sewage ['sju:idʒ]	n.	（下水道里的）污物；污水
petroleum [pə'trəuliəm]	n.	石油
topography [tə'pɔgrəfi]	n.	地形学；地形测量学；地貌
fume [fju:m]	n.	烟雾，气体

disguise [dis'gaiz]	v.	伪装；掩盖，掩饰
	n.	伪装；伪装物
intrusion [in'tru:ʒn]	n.	闯入；打扰；干扰；干涉

【Notes to Text C】

[1] Regional and commuter trains feed cities from suburbs and surrounding areas, while intra-urban transport is performed by high-capacity tramways and rapid transits, often making up the backbone of a city's public transport.

　　tramways　有轨电车
　　rapid transits　高速铁路交通；快轨

[2] Water transport is the process of transport a watercraft, such as a barge, boat, ship or sailboat, makes over a body of water, such as a sea, ocean, lake, canal or river.

　　"process of" 在本句中意为"……的过程"，例如：
　　Growth is a process of trial, error, and experimentation. 成长是一个探索、犯错和实践的过程。
　　"make over" 在本句中意为"航行在……之上"。

[3] For freight, in comparison to sea transport, air transport is expensive for the shipper and the cargo carrying capacity is small.

　　in comparison to　与……相比；同……比较起来
　　carrying capacity　承载能力；载运容量

[4] Short-distance systems exist for sewage, slurry, water and beer, while long-distance networks are used for petroleum and natural gas.

　　be used for　用于；被用于做某事

【Exercises to Text C】

I. Connection work.

```
Natural gas
    Canal              Rail transport              Airport
    Barge
    Aircraft           Road transport              Pumps and valves
    Helicopter
Commuter train         Water transport             Railway station
    Truck
    Bus                Air transport               Seaport
    Slurry
    Automobile         Pipeline transport          Station
    Train
```

II. Play the Snakes and Ladders Game again and try to find the fastest winner.

Chapter 3 Transport Management

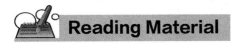 **Reading Material**

Improved Safety and Performance at Lower Cost

Success in the railway industry depends on safety, **reliability**, and **affordability**, with both operators and passengers expecting flawless service—but this requires communications networks that perform to the highest level.

However, radio driver-signaler communication often relies on outdated, analogue radio networks, supplied by multiple vendors. These are expensive to maintain and can only offer limited functionality, often resulting in uncoordinated dispatching.

Huawei addresses these problems using multiple innovative, industry-standard technologies to meet railway communications requirements of the 21st century, offering stability and reliability across various industry-specific signaling standard systems.

Huawei helps to implement a highly reliable, **elastic**, and evolvable end-to-end communications network, covering the three key aspects of railway communications: mission-critical dispatch; system-wide backbone (system-wide interconnection); and broadband trackside devices. Such a network improves safety and reliability yet reduces operational costs, protecting investments made in infrastructure and rolling stock.

Indeed, Huawei innovations are already in use globally—including in Europe, Central Asia, the Middle East, and North Africa—and have proven to consistently improve safety, reducing operating costs and raising overall railway performance.

1. GSM-R Wireless Network Ensures Reliability

Huawei's GSM cellular technology—optimized for Global System for Mobile Communications-Railway (GSM-R)—has the most-comprehensive **redundancy** design in the industry for Network Entities (NEs). Introducing multiple Huawei-proprietary technologies and protection mechanisms, the GSM-R wireless network prevents single points of failure, ensures service security and reliability, and provides robust recovery capabilities in emergency situations.

2. Hybrid MSTP Provides Reliable Networking

Optical Transport Network (OTN) and Multi-Service Transport Platform (MSTP) standards provide the capabilities for implementing Automatically Switched Optical Networks (ASONs) at the rail network's backbone, convergence, and access layers. ASONs are protected using a variety of measures, including Multiplex Section Protection (MSP), Subnetwork Connection Protection (SNCP), and 50-millisecond failover protection.

3. Broadband Transmission Supports Trackside Multi-Service Access

Supporting more than six types of interface—ranging from Foreign Exchange Station (FXS) to GE—Huawei technology handles access for various audio, video, and data services along railway lines, supports emergency rescue, prevents and monitors disasters, audits train safety, supports power system telemechanics, and monitors railway crossings.

【Key Words】

reliability [riˌlaiə'biləti]	n.	可靠性
affordability [əˌfɔːdə'biləti]	n.	支付能力；负担能力；可购性
elastic [i'læstik]	adj.	有弹性的；灵活的；易伸缩的
redundancy [ri'dʌndənsi]	n.	冗余；裁员

【Questions】

Can you give some examples of a company's balancing in the logistical safety and cost?

Chapter 4
Inventory Management

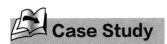

【参考音频】

Why Does an Inventory Error Affect Two Periods?

An **inventory** error affects two periods because: the **ending inventory** of one period will become the **beginning inventory** for the following period; and the calculation of the cost of goods sold is beginning inventory + purchases−ending inventory.

We will demonstrate this with some amounts. Let's assume that a company began on December 1, 2014. During the month of December it **purchased** or manufactured US $100,000 of goods. At the end of December 31, the company reported that its ending inventory was US $15,000. As a result, its balance sheet will report inventory of US $15,000 and its **income**

statement will report cost of goods sold of US $85,000. In January 2015, it purchases US $130,000 of goods and at the end of January 31 it reports inventory of US $20,000. It will report January's cost of goods sold as US $125,000 (beginning inventory of US $15,000 plus purchases of US $130,000 minus ending inventory of US $20,000).

Now let's assume that only one error occurred and it involved the calculation of the December 31 ending inventory. Instead of the US $15,000 that had been reported, the true amount of inventory was US $19,000. That meant the December 31 balance sheet understated the true cost of inventory by US $4,000. It also meant that the income statement's cost of goods sold was not US $85,000. Rather, the true cost of goods sold was US $81,000 (US $100,000 minus US $19,000 of inventory). In January, the true cost of goods sold is US $129,000 (beginning inventory of US $19,000 plus the purchases of US $130,000 minus the January 31 inventory of US $20,000).

To recap, the December 31 balance sheet reported the incorrect ending inventory and the December and January income statements reported the incorrect cost of goods sold, and **gross profit** and net income. The true cost of goods sold for December was US $81,000—not the US $85,000 that was reported. The true cost of goods sold for January was US $129,000—not the US $125,000 that was reported. That one error in calculating the December 31 inventory cost resulted in December's cost of goods sold being too high and January's cost of goods sold being too low. That in turn meant that the reported gross profit for December was US $4,000 too low and January's reported profit was US $4,000 too high.

【Outline】

The case indicates the importance of inventory in a company. Let's learn more about Inventory and management methods.

Chapter 4 Inventory Management

【Key Words】

inventory [ˈinvəntri]	*n.*	存货清单；财产目录，财产目录的编制；存货总值
ending inventory		期末存货
beginning inventory		期初存货
purchase [ˈpɜːtʃəs]	*n.*	购买；采购；购置（purchases 是其复数形式）
income statement		收益表
gross profit		毛利润

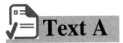

Introduction of Inventory

1. Definition of Inventory Management

Inventory refers to **stocks** of anything necessary to do business.[1] Raw materials, goods in process and finished goods all represent various forms of inventory. Each type represents money tied up until the inventory leaves the organization and is paid for.[2] For this reason it is **undesirable** to hold greater stocks than is necessary.[3] On the other hand, inadequate levels of stock create danger of production hold-ups or failure to meet customer demand.

Unless inventories are controlled, they can be unreliable, inefficient, and costly. Inventory management involves the management of all aspects relating to **stockholding**, with the aim of providing the desired level of customer service at **optimal** cost.[4]

2. The Purpose of Inventory

One reason for having inventory is the convenience of having things available as and when required.[5] What needs to be available will depend on the type of organization or industry but might include:[6]

(1) Production materials (raw materials and components) to support manufacture.[7]

(2) **Spares** and **consumables** for repair and maintenance activities.[8]

(3) Finished products ready for delivery to the final customer.[9]

Another factor is the possibility of cost reduction by taking advantage of **bulk discount** from suppliers. By having in bulk, we accept a relatively high level of stocks in exchange for a reduction in the purchase price.

We may also hold stocks as a buffer against things going wrong.[10] For example, we might hold a high level of finished goods so that we can guarantee to meet customer demand. Similarly, we might hold a high level of raw materials stock so as to avoid any hold-up in the production process.[11]

【参考视频】

3. Inventory Classification

It is important to know the key **classifications** of inventory because the classification influences the way the inventory is managed. Inventory is most frequently classified as cycle (base) stock, safety (buffer) stock, transit (pipeline) stock, speculative stock, and dead stock.

(1) Cycle (base) inventory. Cycle or base stock refers to inventory that is needed to satisfy normal demand during the course of an order cycle, if demand and lead time is constant only cycle stock is necessary.[12]

(2) **Safety (buffer) inventory.** Safety or buffer inventory refers to inventory that is held in addition to cycle stock to guard against **uncertainty** in demand and/or **lead time**.[13] Generally, the higher the level of buffer inventory, the better the firm's customer service. This occurs because the firm suffers fewer "stock-out". Obviously, the better the customer service, the greater the **likelihood** of customer satisfaction.

(3) **Transit inventory**. Transit inventories result from the need to transport items or material from one location to another. Goods shipped by truck or rail can sometimes take days or even weeks to go from a regional warehouse to a retail facility. The increase of transit time for these inventories would lead to an increase in the size of the transit inventory.

(4) **Speculative** inventory. Oftentimes, firms will purchase and hold inventory that is **in excess of** their current need for a possible future event. Such events may include a price increase, a seasonal increase in demand. This **tactic** is commonly used by retailers, who always build up inventory months before the demand for their products will be unusually high (e.g., at Halloween or Christmas).[14]

(5) Dead inventory. Dead inventory refers to product for which there is no demand—at least under current marketing practice. Because dead inventory increases **inventory carrying cost**, reduces inventory **turnover** and takes up inventory space in warehousing facility, companies should minimize the size of dead inventory.[15]

Chapter 4　Inventory Management

【Key Words】

stock [stɔk]	n.	库存；股票；股份
undesirable [ˌʌndiˈzaiərəbl]	adj.	不需要的；不受欢迎的；不方便的
stockholding [ˈstɔkˌhəuldiŋ]	n.	库存控制
optimal [ˈɔptiməl]	adj.	最佳的；最理想的；最优的
spare [speə(r)]	adj.	闲置的；备用的
	n.	备用品；备份
consumable [kənˈsju:məbl]	adj.	可消费的
	n.	消费品
bulk discount		批量折扣
classification [ˌklæsifiˈkeiʃn]	n.	分类，分级；类别；分类系统
safety (buffer) inventory		安全（缓冲）库存
uncertainty [ʌnˈsɜ:tnti]	n.	变化无常；不确定；不确定的事物
lead time		提前期；前置期
likelihood [ˈlaiklihud]	n.	可能，可能性
transit inventory		调节库存
speculative [ˈspekjələtiv]	adj.	投机的；推理的，揣摩的
in excess of		超过
tactic [ˈtæktik]	n.	策略；战略；手段
inventory carrying cost		库存持有成本
turnover [ˈtɜ:nəuvə(r)]	n.	成交量；周转率；营业额

【Notes to Text A】

[1] Inventory refers to stocks of anything necessary to do business.
"necessary to do business" 是形容词结构后置，在句中作定语，修饰 "anything"。
"inventory" 和 "stock" 不同："inventory" 是指 "详细目录；存货，财产清册；总量"，强调的是 "存货总量"；而 "stock" 是指对货物的 "储存"。

[2] Each type represents money tied up until the inventory leaves the organization and is paid for.
"tied up" 是过去分词短语作定语，修饰 "money"，相当于定语从句 "which is tied up"。

[3] For this reason it is undesirable to hold greater stocks than is necessary.
"it" 是形式主语，后面的不定式结构 "to hold…" 是真实主语。
"than is necessary" 是省略语，完整语应为 "than it is necessary"，在口语中也可以直接写为 "than necessary"。

[4] Inventory management involves the management of all aspects relating to stockholding, with the aim of providing the desired level of customer service at optimal cost.
"relating to stockholding" 是 "动词 +ing 短语" 作定语的用法，修饰名词 "aspects"，相当于定语从句 "which relate to"。
"with the aim of" 意为 "目的是……"。

[5] One reason for having inventory is the convenience of having things available as and when required.

"having inventory"和"having things available"是两个"动词+ing"短语，分别作介词"for"和"of"的宾语。

"as and when required"意为"按照所需并在需要的时候"，这仅是英语的一个通用的表达方法，实际翻译时译为"在需要时"即可，否则句子就会显得臃肿。

[6] What needs to be available will depend on the type of organization or industry but might include:

"what needs to be available"引导的是一个主语从句。

"depend on"本意为"依靠……，信赖……"，这里意为"取决于……"，例如：

Whether we leave or not will depend on the weather condition. 我们是否动身将取决于天气情况。

[7] Production materials (raw materials and components) to support manufacture.

"to support manufacture"是介词短语，起到修饰形容词的作用。

[8] Spares and consumables for repair and maintenance activities.

"for repair and maintenance activities"是介词短语，起到起修饰名词的作用。

[9] Finished products ready for delivery to the final customer.

"ready for…"是形容词短语后置作定语的用法，修饰"finished products"。

[10] We may also hold stocks as a buffer against things going wrong.

"a buffer against…"意为"应对……的一种缓冲或缓解"。

"against things going wrong"相当于"against things which may go wrong"。

[11] …so as to avoid any hold-up in the production process.

"so as to"相当于"in order"，意为"以便，以致"。

"hold-up"也作"holdup"，意为"（某事在进行中的）停顿，耽搁；（交通）堵塞"等。

[12] Cycle or base stock refers to inventory that is needed to satisfy normal demand during the course of an order cycle, if demand and lead time is constant only cycle stock is necessary.

"that is needed to satisfy normal demand during the course of an order cycle"是定语从句，修饰"inventory"。

"if demand and lead time is constant only cycle stock is necessary"是状语从句。

[13] Safety or buffer inventory refers to inventory that is held in addition to cycle stock to guard against uncertainty in demand and/or lead time.

"to guard against"是一个动词不定式结构作目的状语。

"that is held in addition to cycle stock"是定语从句，修饰"inventory"。

[14] This tactic is commonly used by retailers, who always build up inventory months before the demand for their products will be unusually high (e.g., at Halloween or Christmas).

"who always build up inventory months before the demand for their products will be unusually high (e.g., at Halloween, Christmas)"是定语从句，其中"before"是介词，充当时间状语。

[15] Because dead inventory increases inventory carrying cost, reduces inventory turnover and takes up space in warehousing facility, companies should minimize the size of dead inventory.

"because…"是原因状语从句，意为"因为……所以……"。

Chapter 4 Inventory Management

【Exercises to Text A】

I. Fill in the blanks.

Companies often underestimate how much waste actually costs—did you know, for example, that it could be up to 4 percent of your ___1___? All of the waste that you produce has a cost associated with it, but before you can begin reducing waste you need to ___2___ where it comes from.

Lack of appropriate ___3___ costs companies heavily, not only in terms of ___4___, but also the long-term impacts on the environment and sustainability. It is important to ___5___ that the true cost of waste is more than just the cost of disposal. It also includes the additional cost of raw materials, energy and labour ___6___ in the generation of waste. All together this can be 5—20 times higher than the cost of disposal.

As well as the ___7___, effective waste management helps organizations to become compliant with increasingly ___8___ legislation designed to ___9___ the environmental impact of landfill sites.

Effective waste management offers ___10___ benefits to companies including:

(1) Cost savings (reduced raw material consumption, reduced ___11___ cost savings due to reduced volumes and recovered value of wastes) that go directly to the bottom line.

(2) A competitive advantage.

(3) Reduced impact to environment.

(4) Improved public perception.

(5) Development of new and more sustainable processes.

(6) Development of new products.

The waste hierarchy ___12___ possible waste disposal options and ranks them ___13___ increasing environmental impact. The aim is to work your way up the hierarchy from disposal until you end up ___14___ all waste where possible.

The way that you currently deal with waste will ___15___ the stage you are at on the hierarchy. Organizations should aspire to work their way up the hierarchy with the aim of turning the 4 per cent of turnover into profit.

II. Reading and answering questions.

There are three types of stock that a business can hold:

(1) Stocks of raw materials (inputs brought from suppliers waiting to be used in the production process).

(2) Work in progress (incomplete products still in the process of being made).

(3) Stocks of finished products (finished goods of acceptable quality waiting to be sold to customers).

The aim of stock control is to minimize the cost of holding these stocks whilst ensuring that there are enough materials for production to continue and be able to meet customer demand. Obtaining the correct balance is not easy and the stock control department will work closely with the purchasing and marketing departments.

The marketing department should be able to provide sales forecasts for the coming weeks or months (this can be difficult if demand is seasonal or prone to unexpected fluctuation) and so allow stock control managers to judge the type, quantity and timing of stocks needed.

It is the purchasing department's responsibility to order the correct quantity and quality of these inputs, at a competitive price and from a reliable supplier who will deliver on time.

As it is difficult to ensure that a business has exactly the correct amount of stock at any one time, the majority of firms will hold buffer stock. This is the "safe" amount of stock that needs to be held to cover unforeseen rises in demand or problems of reordering supplies.

Good stock management by a firm will lower costs, improve efficiency and ensure production can meet fluctuations in customer demand. It will give the firm a competitive advantage as more efficient production can feed through to lower prices and also customers should always be satisfied as products will be available on demand.

However, poor stock control can lead to problems associated with overstocking or stock-outs.

If a firm holds too much buffer stock (stock held in reserve) or overestimates the level of demand for its products, then it will overstock. Overstocking increases costs for businesses as holding stocks is an expense for firms for several reasons:

(1) Increases warehouse space needed.

(2) Higher insurance costs needed.

(3) Higher security costs needed to prevent theft.

(4) Stocks may be damaged, become obsolete or perish (go out of date).

(5) Money spent buying the stocks could have been better spent elsewhere.

The opposite of an overstock is a stock-out. This occurs when a business runs out of stocks. This can have severe consequences for the business:

(1) Loss of production (with workers still having to be paid but no products being produced).

(2) Potential loss of sales or missed orders. This can harm the reputation of the business.

In these circumstances a firm may choose to increase the amount of stock it holds in reserve (buffer stock). There are advantages and disadvantages of increasing the stock level.

Advantages	Disadvantages
Can meet sudden changes in demand	Costs of storage—rent and insurance
Less chance of loss of production time because of stock outs	Money tied up in stocks not being used elsewhere in the business
Can take advantage of bulk buying economies of scale	Large stocks subject to deterioration and theft

Questions:

1. The aim of stock control is (   ).

    A. to minimize the cost of holding stocks and ensure production

    B. to order the correct quantity and quality of stocks

    C. to provide sales forecasts for the coming weeks or months

    D. to judge the type, quantity and timing of stocks needed

2. The word "buffer" in Line 19 probably means (   ).

    A. protection   B. quantity   C. reserve   D. insurance

3. The costs of overstocking include the following except (   ).

    A. increases warehouse space and higher insurance costs needed

    B. potential loss of sales or missed orders

    C. higher security costs needed to prevent theft

    D. stocks may be damaged, become obsolete or perish

4. Which of the following is one of the advantages of increasing the stock level? (   )
   A. costs of storage, rent and insurance
   B. less chance of loss of production time because of stock-outs
   C. money tied up in stocks not being used elsewhere in the business
   D. large stocks subject to deterioration and theft
5. Which of the following is not discussed in the passage? (   )
   A. the types of stocks   B. the purpose of stock control
   C. the importance of stock control   D. the methods of stock control

III. Translation.

1. The inventory requirements of a firm depend on the network structure and the desired level of customer service.

2. Similarly, transport vehicles break down, raw materials may suddenly be unavailable.

3. For all of these reasons, inventory is utilized to ensure that customer needs are met even when the production process itself interrupted.

4. The finished products can be shipped to field warehouses where they are mixed to fill customer order.

5. Excessive inventories may compensate for deficiencies in basic design of a logistics network and to some degree inferior management.

Text B

Principles of Inventory

1. ABC Analysis of Inventory

Firms that carry hundreds or even thousands of different parts can be faced with the impossible task of monitoring the inventory levels of every single part. To solve this problem, many firms use an ABC analysis of inventory. This **approach** recognizes that inventories are not of equal value to a firm and that, as a result, all inventory should not be managed in the same way.[1] According to ABC analysis, 20 percent of all inventory items represent 80 percent of inventory costs. Therefore, a firm can control 80 percent of its inventory costs by monitoring and controlling 20 percent of its inventory. But, it has to be the correct 20 percent.[2]

The top 20 percent of the firm's most costly items are termed "A" items (this should **approximately** represent 80 percent of total inventory costs). Items that are extremely inexpensive or have low demand are termed "C", with "B" items falling in between A and C items. B items usually represent about 30 percent of the total inventory items and 15 percent of the costs. C items generally consist 50 percent of all inventory items but only around 5 percent of the costs (see Table 4-1).

Table 4-1 ABC analysis

	A	B	C
Item	5%～10%	15%～25%	25%～85%
Value	70%～85%	10%～20%	5%～10%
Inventory control	Tight	Normal	Minimal
Data accuracy	High	Reasonable	Low
Review of usage rate and demand	Frequent	Occasional	Waived sometimes
Cycle counting	Frequent	Less frequent but regular	Minimal

By **classifying** each inventory item as an A, B or C, the firm can determine the resources (time, effort and money) to each item. Usually this means that the firm monitors A items very closely but can check on B and C items on a **periodic** basis (for example, monthly for B items and **quarterly** for C items).[3]

2. Economic Order Quantity

The EOQ is the replenishment practice that **minimizes** the combined inventory carrying and ordering cost.[4] **Identification** of such a quantity assumes that demand and costs are relatively stable throughout the year. Since EOQ is calculated on an individual product basis, the basic **formulation** does not consider the impact of joint ordering of products.[5]

Chapter 4 Inventory Management

The most efficient method for calculating EOQ is mathematical. A policy **dilemma** regarding whether to order 100, 200, or 600 units was discussed. The answer can be found by calculating the applicable EOQ for the situation.

To make the appropriate calculations, the standard formulation for EOQ is:

$$EOQ=\sqrt{\frac{2CD}{KU}}$$

Where EOQ=economic order quantity;

C=cost per order;

D=annual sales volume, units;

K=annual inventory carrying cost per Unit;

U=cost per unit.

Substituting from Table 4-2:

$$EOQ=\sqrt{\frac{2\times 2,400\times 19}{0.2\times 5}}=302\approx 300$$

Table 4-2 Factors of determining EOQ

Annual demand volume	2,400 units
Unit value at cost	US $5.00
Inventory carrying cost percent	20% annually
Ordering cost	US $19.00 per order

------ ••••• ------

【Key Words】

approach [əˈprəutʃ]	n.	方法；途径；接近；步骤
approximately [əˈprɔksimətli]	adv.	近似；大约
classify [ˈklæsifai]	vt.	将……分类（classifying 的现在分词）
periodic [ˌpiəriˈɔdik]	adj.	周期的；定期的；间歇的
quarterly [ˈkwɔːtəli]	adj.	季度的；四分之一
	n.	季刊；季考
economic order quantity		经济订货量；最佳订货量
minimize [ˈminimaiz]	vt.	将……减到最小
identification [aiˌdentifiˈkeiʃn]	n.	身体证明；识别
formulation [ˌfɔːmjuˈleiʃn]	n.	配方；规划；公式化
dilemma [diˈlemə]	n.	困境；进退两难
substituting [ˈsʌbstitjuːtiŋ]	n.	取代；代替（substitute 的现在分词）

【Notes to Text B】

[1] This approach recognizes that inventories are not of equal value to a firm and that, as a result, all inventory should not be managed in the same way.

"recognizes that…" 是一个宾语从句，意为"认为……"。

"are not of equal value" 这个短语意为"价值不等同"。

[2] Therefore, a firm can control 80 percent of its inventory costs by monitoring and controlling 20 percent of its inventory. But, it has to be the correct 20 percent.

"therefore" 是副词，引出后面的句子；"but" 是连词，起转折的作用。

[3] Usually this means that the firm monitors A items very closely but can check on B and C items on a periodic basis (for example, monthly for B items and quarterly for C items).

"this means that…" 是宾语从句，通常用来陈述一个观点。

[4] The EOQ is the replenishment practice that minimizes the combined inventory carrying and ordering cost.

"that minimizes the combined inventory carrying and ordering cost" 是定语从句，"that minimizes the combined inventory carrying and ordering cost" 修饰 "practice"。

[5] Since EOQ is calculated on an individual product basis, the basic formulation does not consider the impact of joint ordering of products.

"since" 引出原因状语从句，意为"因为……所以……"。

【Exercises to Text B】

I. Translation.

1. The typical measures of inventory commitment are time duration, depth, and width of commitment.

2. A wholesaler purchases large quantities from manufacturers and sells smaller quantities to retailers.

3. Due to the high cost of store location, retailers place prime emphasis on inventory turnover and direct product profitability.

4. Faced with this width of inventory, retailers attempt to reduce risk by pressing manufacturers and wholesalers to assume greater and greater inventory responsibility.

5. Stock-out(shortages) can be completely avoided if orders are placed at right time.

6. In other words, the production schedule "pulls" components through the system in order to the manufacturing needs.

7. DRP is a more sophisticated planning approach that considers multiple distribution stages and the characteristics of each stage.

II. Reading and answering questions.

It can be argued that, over the last few years, the real value of trade credit has not been fully recognized. Many companies have had a strong cash flow and this, allied with a benign economic climate and steady level of corporate failures, has reduced the risk associated with trading on credit. However, the changing economic climate means that confidence in granting credit is reducing, leading to an increasing interest in credit insurance.

The cause of this has been the repricing of risk triggered by the well publicised Sub-Prime lending defaults in the U.S.A., resulting in a shortage of finance and volatility in the stock markets, with US Sub-Prime delinquent debt rising at an alarming rate. For example, in the U.S.A. in 2003 four percent of debt defaulted after an average of 48 months. In 2006, this default figure had risen to ten percent and the average default time fallen to 12 months.

Much of this debt is ultimately owned by major financial institutions and a knock-on effect has been the reduced amount of credit available to the corporate sector.

That this increasing difficulty in obtaining additional/temporary bank funding has occurred now is particularly worrying, as quarter four into quarter one is traditionally the worst period of the year for corporate insolvencies, and a restriction in the availability of funds could increase this figure, leading to an increase in bad debt. One impact of this is that terms of payment will get longer and the cost of funding this will be tough; too tough for some. Atradius (one of the UK's largest credit insurers) have already seen requests to push terms out from 60 days and 150 days.

To compete in a competitive market sector companies need to offer credit. They also need to protect their credit risk as much as possible and manage the sales ledger cycle, so they can be confident that bad debt will not impact upon their ability to trade.

Credit Insurance provides between 80 percent—100 percent cover against the non-payment of commercial debts due to the insolvency or default of an insured customer. Companies can choose whether to insure just their export ledger, UK ledger, top accounts, selected markets/buyers or any combination. It is backed by a credit limit service and sometimes a debt collection service. Cost is calculated using a number of differing factors including previous bad debt experience, level of projected sales, trade sectors and deductibles. Willis Credit Risks are able to assess the potential credit risk within a company and offer advice on possible solutions to reducing that overall risk.

Credit Insurance can literally save the life of a company. A glazing company in the North East was hit by a number of bad debts which had a potentially catastrophic impact on their cash flow. However, they had taken out credit insurance and were able to claim on their policy. As the Finance Director of the company said at the time, "Without credit insurance we would not have been able to replace our working capital as quickly as we did following a number of insolvency losses we suffered in 2006. Credit insurance allowed our funders to remain confident in our business plan and without this insurance our prospects of continued trading would have been slim."

Questions:

1. The word "default" in Para. 2 is closest in meaning to "(   )".
   A. degrade　　　　　B. delicate　　　　　C. delinquent　　　D. decrease
2. According to the passage, what may cause an increase in bad debt? (   )
   A. restriction in the availability of funds
   B. difficulty in obtaining additional/temporary bank funding
   C. the reduced amount of credit available to the corporate sector
   D. both A and B
3. Atradius is a company that (   ).
   A. owns many debts　　　　　　　　B. provides credit insurance
   C. helps to collect debts　　　　　　D. buys credit insurance
4. Credit Insurance provides services in the following field except (   ).
   A. export ledger　　　　　　　　　B. top accounts
   C. selected markets/buyers　　　　　D. bank funding
5. Which of the following statements best describes the main idea of the passage? (   )
   A. Credit Insurance is very important in helping a company to protect its credit risk.
   B. The changing economic climate led to an increasing interest in credit insurance.
   C. Credit Insurance saved the life of a glazing company in the North East.
   D. Credit Insurance provides cover against the non-payment of commercial debts.

Reading Material A

JIT① Inventory Management

1. Introduction of JIT

In the early 1970s, Toyota Motor Manufacturing developed a new production strategy that used little inventory, shortened cycle times, improved quality, and eliminated waste and costs in the supply chain.

---

① JIT　Just In Time 的缩写，即准时制生产方式，又称无库存生产方式或者超级市场生产方式。

Chapter 4 Inventory Management

This JIT manufacturing management requires manufacturers to work in concert with suppliers and transportation providers to get required items to the assembly line at the exact time they are needed for production. The concept was also adopted by American and European automakers in response to the growing success of their Japanese competitors. The JIT concept then spread to other industries such as computers, and became popular in manufacturing strategies around the world.

2. JIT Concept

JIT is a **philosophy** of continuous and forced problem solving. With JIT, supplies and components are "pulled" through a system to arrive where they are needed when they are needed. When goods units do not arrive just as needed, a "problem" has been identified. This makes JIT an excellent tool to help operations managers add value by driving out waste and unwanted variability. Because there is no excess inventory or excess time in a JIT system, costs from unneeded inventory are eliminated and throughput improved. Consequently, the benefits of JIT are particularly helpful in supporting strategies of rapid response and low cost.

3. Advantages of JIT

(1) More **inventory turns**. Because there is less stock on hand, the inventory that is maintained stays for a shorter period of time.

(2) Better quality. As was mentioned earlier, high quality products must be received with a JIT system, otherwise the entire benefit production process collapses.

(3) Less warehouse space needed. When there is less inventory, fewer and/or smaller warehouses are required.

4. Disadvantages of JIT

(1) Risk of **stock-outs**. When firms eliminate inventory, the risk of stocking out can rise. Managers attempt to minimize this occurrence by demanding very high levels of service from their vendors and logistics service providers.

(2) Increased purchasing costs. Purchasing **discounts** are generally associated with buying large quantities at one time. Theoretically, JIT means foregoing those **price-breaks** in favor of obtaining smaller amounts more frequently.

(3) Small channel members may suffer. JIT is sometimes criticized as a system that allows strong organizations to shift their inventory to smaller firms in the channel.

(4) Environmental issues. JIT can lead to higher levels of traffic congestion and air pollution because additional transportation is often required to maintain customer service levels in the absence of inventory.

5. Zero Inventory

JIT tactics are still being incorporated in manufacturing to improve quality, drive down inventory investment, and reduce other costs. However, JIT is also established practice in restaurants, where customers expect it, and a **necessity** in the produce business, where there is little choice.

Pacific Pre-Cut Produce, a US $14 million fruit and vegetable processing company in Tracy, California, holds inventory to zero. Buyers are in action in the very early hours of the morning. At 6 a.m., production crews show up. Orders for very specific cuts and mixtures of fruit and vegetable salads and **stir-fry ingredients** for supermarkets, restaurants, and institutional kitchens pour in from 8 a.m. until 4 p.m. .

Shipping begins at 10 p.m. and continues until the last order is filled and loaded at 5 a.m. the next morning. Inventories are once again zero, things are relatively quiet, and then the routine starts again. The company has accomplished a complete cycle of purchase, manufacture, and shipping in about 24 hours. VP Bob Borzone calls the process the ultimate in **mass-customization**. "We buy everything as a bulk commodity, then slice and dice it to fit the exact requirements of the end user. There are 20 different stir-fry mixes. Some customers want the snow peas clipped on both ends, some just on one. Some want only red bell peppers in the mix, some only yellow. You tailor the product to the customer's requirements. You're trying to the need of a lot of end users, and each restaurant and retailer wants to look different."

【Key Words】

philosophy [fəˈlɔsəfi]	n.	哲学；哲学思想；生活信条
inventory turns		库存周转
stock-outs	n.	缺货
discounts [ˈdiskaʊnts]	n.	贴现；数目；扣除额（discount 的复数形式）
price-breaks	n.	梯度价
zero inventory		零库存
necessity [nəˈsesəti]	n.	必需品；必要，需要
stir-fry ingredients		翻炒配料
mass-customization	n.	大规模定制

Chapter 4　Inventory Management

【Questions】

1. Can JIT strategy be applied to service industry?
2. Which advantages does JIT involve?
3. What are the disadvantages of JIT?
4. How can the manufacturer keep zero inventory?

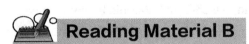

New Trend of Inventory Management

1. MRP①

How does MRP work? MRP deals specifically with supplying materials and component parts whose demand depends upon the demand for a specific end product. **Essentially**, MRP begins by determining how much of the final product customers desire, and when they need it. Then MRP breaks down the timing and need for components (all of which could have different lead times) based upon that scheduled end-product need. An MRP system consists of a set of logically related procedures, decision rules, and records, which are designed to translate a master production schedule into time-phased net inventory also re-plans net requirements as a result of changes.

MRP minimizes inventory **to the extent** that the master production schedule accurately reflects what is needed to satisfy customer demand. If the production schedule does not match demand, the company will have too much of some items and too little of others. Because the master production schedule drives the need for parts, MRP is said to be a **pull system**. In other words,

---

① MRP　Material Requirements Planning 的缩写，即物料需求计划。

the production schedule "pulls" components through the system in order to meet manufacturing needs.

2. DRP[①]

DRP is a more **sophisticated** planning approach that considers multiple distribution stages and the characteristics of each stage. DRP is the logical extension of manufacturing requirements planning, although there is one fundamental difference between the two techniques.

MRP is determined by a production schedule that is defined and controlled by the enterprise. On the other hand, DRP is guided by customer demand, which is not controllable by the enterprise. So, while MRP generally operates in a dependent demand situation, DRP operates in an independent environment where uncertain customer demand determines inventory requirements. The MRP component coordinates the scheduling and integration of materials into finished goods. MRP controls inventory until manufacturing or assembly is completed. DRP then takes **coordination** responsibility once finished goods are received in the plant warehouse.

【Key Words】

essentially [i'senʃəli]	adv.	本质上，根本上；本来
to the extent		到……的程度
pull system		拉动系统
sophisticated [sə'fistikeitid]	adj.	复杂的；精致的；富有经验的
	v.	使变得世故；使迷惑（sophisticate 的过去分词）
coordination [kəuˌɔːdi'neiʃn]	n.	协调；配合

【Questions】

1. What is MRP?
2. What does MRP system consist of?
3. What is the distinction between DRP and MRP?

---

① DRP Distribution Requirements Planning 的缩写，即分销需求计划。

Chapter 5
Warehouse Management

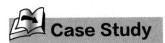

Public Bonded Warehouse

　　Recently a public **bonded warehouse** has been set up in the District B of International Logistics Center (the second section), which is the first public bonded warehouse in Yiwu. The bonded warehouse has an area of 5,184 square meters with a **supplementary** loading area of 650.5 square meters.The warehouse is for the storage of bonded goods and goods whose **customs formalities** have not been completed, mainly including goods for export with materials provided by customers, goods for export with imported materials, and goods to be exported again after a temporary delay. Besides, it also deals with other businesses, including approving the **consignment** sales, fast transfer and exhibition of bonded goods.

【Outline】

Please illustrate types of warehouse.

【Key Words】

bonded warehouse		保税仓库；关栈仓库
supplementary [ˌsʌpliˈmentri]	adj.	增补的，追加的
customs formalities		报关单；海关手续
consignment [kənˈsainmənt]	n.	托运，运送；委托，托管；装运（托运）的货物

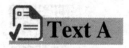 Text A

Types of Warehousing

Warehousing is an **integral** part of a logistics system. There are estimated 750,000 warehouse **facilities** worldwide, including professionally managed warehouses, and company **stockrooms**, garages and even garden sheds. When a firm decides to store product, it faces two warehousing options: rented facilities, called public warehousing, or owned or leased facilities, called private warehousing.[1]

Firms must examine closely to choose between the two options. For example, the price of a public warehouse is most probably higher because it will be operated at a profit; it may also have selling and advertising cost.[2] However, a firm makes no initial investment in the facilities. For customer service, private warehousing can generally provide higher service levels because of its more specialized facilities and equipment, and its better **familiarity** with the firm's products, customers and market. In some instances, **innovative** public warehouses can provide higher levels of service owning to their expertise and strong **competitive drive** to serve the customer.[3]

【参考视频】

In the following, we will discuss about public warehousing. There are many types of public warehouses, including:

1. General Merchandise Warehouse

The general merchandise warehouse is probably the most common form. It is designed to be used by manufacturers, distributors, and customers for storing almost any kind of product.

2. Refrigerated Warehouses

Refrigerated or cold storage warehouses provide a **temperature-controlled** storage environment. They tend to be used for preserving perishable items such as fruits and vegetables. However, a number of other items (e.g., frozen food products, some **pharmaceuticals, photographic paper** and film, and furs) require this type of facility.[4]

3. Special Commodity Warehouses

Special commodity warehouses are used for particular agricultural products, such as grains, wool, and cotton. Ordinarily each of these warehouses handles one kind of product and offers special services specific to that product.

4. Bonded Warehouses

Some general merchandise or special commodity warehouses are known as bonded warehouses. <u>Goods such as imported tobacco and alcoholic beverages are stored in this type of warehouse, although the government retains control of the goods until they are distributed to the market place.</u>[5] The advantage of the bonded warehouse is that the import duties need not be paid until the merchandise is sold, so that the importer has the funds on hand to pay these fees.

5. Bulk Storage Warehouses

Bulk storage warehouses provide tank storage of liquids and open or sheltered storage of dry products such as coal, sand, and chemicals.

······

【Key Words】

integral ['intigrəl]	adj.	完整的
facilities [fə'silitiz]	n.	设施；设备；工具（faciliey 的复数形式）
stockroom ['stɔkru:m]	n.	储藏室；仓库
familiarity [fəˌmili'ærəti]	n.	熟悉；通晓
innovative ['inəveitiv]	adj.	创新的；革新的
competitive drive		竞争驱动力
temperature-controlled	adj.	温控的
pharmaceutical [ˌfɑ:mə'su:tikl]	n.	药品
	adj.	制药的；配药的
photographic paper		相纸

【Notes to Text A】

[1] When a firm decides to store product, it faces two warehousing options: rented facilities, called public warehousing, or owned or leased facilities, called private warehousing.

"rented" 意为 "租赁的"；"facilities" 意为 "设施，设备"；"warehousing" 意为 "仓储"。

[2] For example, the price of a public warehouse is most probably higher because it will be operated at a profit; it may also have selling and advertising cost.

"at a profit" 意为 "在获取一定利润的基础上"。

"because" 表示 "……的原因是……" 这一意义时，一般要用到这样的句型：The reason why he can't come is that he is tired. 他不能来是因为他累了。在这一结构中，尽管不少人认为可将 "that" 改用 "because"，但也有不少人反对这一用法，所以要慎用。

[3] In some instances, innovative public warehouses can provide higher levels of service owning to their expertise and strong competitive drive to serve the customer.

"innovative" 意为 "创新的"；"expertise" 意为 "专业知识和技术"。

"in some instances" 在某些情况下，引导后面的句子。

[4] However, a number of other items (e.g., frozen food products, some pharmaceuticals, photographic paper and film, and furs) require this type of facility.

Chapter 5　Warehouse Management

"however"作副词用时，表示"然而，但是"，可以位于句首、句中和句末：位于句首时，要用逗号与句子其他部分隔开；位于句中时，其前后都要用逗号；位于句末时，其前用逗号分开。例如：

She felt ill. She went to work, however, and tried to concentrate. 她病了，然而她依旧去上班，并且尽力集中精神工作。

[5] Goods such as imported tobacco and alcoholic beverages are stored in this type of warehouse, although the government retains control of the goods until they are distributed to the market place.

"retains"意为"保持"；"distributed"意为"分销的"。

"although"比较正式，语气较强，其引导的从句放在主句前后均可，有时可放在句中。例如：

Although he was tired, he went on working. 虽然很累，但是他坚持工作。

Although many difficulties are still ahead, we are determined to make greater achievements. 尽管在前进的道路上还有许多困难，但是我们决心要取得更大的成就。

"although"不能指假设的情况，不能作并列连词，也不能作副词放在词尾。

【Exercises to Text A】

I. Choose the best answer.

1. The most important facility used in warehousing is (　　).
   A. warehouse　　　　　　　　　B. storage
   C. conveyor　　　　　　　　　　D. carousel

2. (　　) are more flexible because the enterprises have authority over all the activities in the warehouse.
   A. Private warehouses　　　　　B. Public warehouses
   C. Contract warehouses　　　　D. all of the above

3. A bonded warehouse is a (　　).
   A. private warehouse　　　　　B. public warehouse
   C. contract warehouse　　　　D. none of the above

4. (　　) can provide unique and specially tailored warehousing services to the customers.
   A. Private warehouses　　　　　B. Public warehouses
   C. Contract warehouses　　　　D. all of the above

II. Translation.

Job title (岗位): Foreman (仓库主管)
Department (部门): Warehouse (仓库)

Responsibilities
1. Arrange the warehouse daily work and control the process to assure the production going well.
2. Audit and revise the work procedure and management system and keep improving.
3. Hold business training and assessment for members to improve the workers' quality and efficiency.
4. In charge of warehouse HR plan and management and distribute reasonable HR.
5. In charge of all the equipment's maintenance.
6. Supervise and check warehouse "6S".
7. Assure the warehouse target consistent with company development strategy.
8. Be responsible for warehouse safety production and fire protection.

Continued

Requirements

1. More than 4-year experience in the warehouse of large enterprises, more than 2-year warehouse foreman experience.
2. Graduated from high school or above.
3. Familiar with Microsoft office.
4. Familiar with internal delivery procedure.
5. Strong communication ability and have spirit as team.
6. Open-minded, creative.
7. Careful and active to the work and strong sense of safety production.

III. Reading and answering questions.

Lately, the question running through my mind has been, "What's in your supply chain?"

In just the past few months, toy companies have had to recall products made overseas because their suppliers used lead paint, which can be very harmful to children. Pet food manufacturers have had to recall products after dogs died, because an overseas supplier used a harmful chemical in the food. Then, last week came reports that people in the United States and Germany were getting ill from heparin, possibly because of tainted supplies coming from China. And General Mills, Nestlé and ConAgra Foods had to ask supermarkets to remove some of their products affected by the recall of meat from the Westland/Hallmark Meat Packing Co. in Chino, Calif.

These unfortunate incidents underscore the challenges companies face in an increasingly integrated global supply chain. Walmart and other retailers are being sued over the dog food poisonings, even though they were not the parties at fault—rather, an importer had reportedly changed the labels to hide the fact that potentially harmful ingredients had been used.

Companies are going to increasingly demand more information from their suppliers to protect themselves from lawsuits, their brands from negative publicity, and the public from harm. And if they don't, governments will demand more information from them. The U.S. Senate passed a tough measure last week that will require a higher number of inspections of toys by the Consumer Products Safety Commission.

We are moving inexorably toward a world where everything in the supply chain is being more closely tracked. Radio frequency identification is going to be a greater part of that over time, but 2D bar code can also be employed to capture serialized information about parts and materials that are going into products.

Clearly, we're going to see a rapid rise in the adoption of automatic identification technologies over the next decade. These technologies could provide information on what suppliers are doing and what's going into their supplies, as well as reduce counterfeiting. But auto-ID technologies can only help if the data collected can be turned into actionable information and shared with business partners.

That's why I'm such a strong believer in standards—and not just within the RFID industry. I believe we need to develop standards that will enable any data collected automatically—whether by a passive RFID, active real-time location, 2D bar code, ZigBee or Wi-Fi system—to be employed across supply chains, across borders and among trading partners.

That shouldn't be that difficult to achieve. If data can be output from these systems in a format compliant with EPCglobal's EPC Information Services standard, companies can use the data and software to create new applications, or modify existing applications to take advantage of all the data captured. That's what we should be working toward, because it's the only way you'll ever know what's in your supply chain.

Chapter 5 Warehouse Management

Questions:
1. According to the passage, (   ) is being sued over dog food poisoning.
   A. General Mills   B. Nestlé
   C. ConAgra Foods   D. Walmart
2. Companies have to recall products made overseas because (   ).
   A. suppliers used harmful ingredients in the products
   B. their products are of low quality
   C. they want to protect their business information
   D. they want to change the labels on the products
3. Companies are going to demand more information from their suppliers to (   ).
   A. protect themselves from lawsuits
   B. protect their brands from negative publicity
   C. protect the public from harm
   D. all of the above
4. The adoption of automatic identification technologies can (   ).
   A. provide information about parts and materials that are going into products
   B. develop standards that will enable any data collected automatically
   C. create new applications, or modify existing applications to all the products
   D. help to remove harmful ingredients from the supply chain
5. The main idea of the passage is that companies need to (   ).
   A. keep track on parts and materials used in their products
   B. recall their products which used poisoning materials
   C. demand more information from their suppliers
   D. collect data across supply chains and among their suppliers

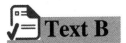

Warehouse Equipment

Modern warehouses employ a wide range of handling equipment. <u>The type of equipment most used is **forklift trucks**, walking-rider **pallet trucks, towlines, tractor-trailer devices, conveyors** and so on.</u>[1] They are described as following.

1. Forklift Trucks

Forklift trucks can move loads of **master cartons** both horizontally and vertically. A pallet or slip sheet forms a platform upon which master cartons are stacked. A slip sheet consists of a thin sheet of material such as **solid fiber** or **corrugated paper. Slip sheets** are an inexpensive alternative to pallets and are ideal for situations which product is handled only a few times. A forklift truck normally transports a maximum of two unit loads (two pallets) at a time. However, forklifts are not limited to unit-load handling. Skids or boxes may also be transported depending on the nature of the product.

Many types of forklift trucks are available, high-stacking trucks capable of up to 40 feet of vertical movement, pallet less side-clamp versions, and trucks capable of operating in aisles as 56 inches can be found in logistical warehouses.[2] Particular attention to narrow-aisle trucks has increased in recent years, as warehouses seek to increase **rack storage density** and overall storage capacity. The forklift truck is not economical for long-distance horizontal movement because of the high ratio of labor per unit of transfer. Therefore, forklift trucks are most effectively utilized in shipping and receiving, and to place merchandise in high cube storage. The two most common power sources for forklifts are propane gas and electricity.

2. Walking-rider Pallet Trucks

Walking-rider pallet trucks provide a low-cost, effective method material-handling utility. Typical applications include loading and unloading, **order selection** and **accumulation**, and **shuttling** loads over longer transportation distances throughout the warehouse. Electricity is the typical power source.

3. Towlines

Towlines consist of either in-floor or overhead-mounted drag devices.[3] They are utilized in combination with four-wheel trailers on a continuous power basis. The main advantage of a towline is continuous movement. However, such handling devices do not have the flexibility of forklift. The most common application of towlines is for order selection within the warehouse. Order selectors place merchandise on a four-wheel trailer, which is then towed to the shipping dock.[4] A number of automated **decoupling** devices have been perfected that route trailers from the main line to selected shipping docks.

A point of debate involves the relative merits of in-floor and overhead towline installation. In-floor installation is costly to modify and difficult to maintain from a housekeeping viewpoint. Overhead installation is more flexible, but unless the warehouse floor is absolutely level, the line may jerk the front wheels of the trailers off the ground and risk product damage.

4. Tow Tractor with Trailers

A tow tractor with trailer consists of a driver-guided power unit towing a number of individual four-wheel "trailers" that hold several palletized loads. The typical size of the trailers is 4 by 8 feet. The tow tractor with trailer, like the towline, is typically used to support order selection. The main advantage of tow tractor with trailers is flexibility. It is not as economical as the towline because of requires greater labor participation and is often idle. Considerable advancements have been made in **automated-guided vehicle systems** (AGVS).

5. Conveyors

Conveyors are used widely in shipping and receiving operations and form the basic handling device for a number of order selection systems. Conveyors are classified according to power, gravity, roller or belt movement. In power systems, the conveyor uses a drive chain from either above or below. Considerable conveyor flexibility is **sacrificed** in such power **configuration** installations. Gravity and roller or belt systems permit the basic installation to be modified with minimum difficulty. **Portable gravity-style** roller conveyors are often used at the warehouse for loading and unloading and, in some cases, are transported on **over-the-road trailers** to assist in unloading at the destination.[5]

【Key Words】

forklift trucks		叉车
pallet trucks		平板卡车
towline ['təʊlain]	n.	拖绳，拖链；纤
tractor-trailer devices		牵引式挂车运输设备
conveyor [kən'veiə(r)]	n.	输送机；运送者
master cartons		硬纸板箱
solid fiber		致密纤维板
corrugated paper		瓦楞纸
slip sheets		薄衬纸
rack storage density		货架存储密度
order selection		订单拣选
accumulation [ə‚kju:mjə'leiʃən]	n.	堆积（物）；积聚；堆放
shuttling ['ʃʌtliŋ]	v.	穿梭移动；往返运送（shuttle 的现在分词）
decoupling [di'kʌpliŋ]	n.	去耦合装置
automated-guided vehicle systems		自动导引小车系统
sacrificed ['sækrifaist]	vt.	牺牲；献出（sacrifice 的过去分词）
configuration [kən‚figə'reiʃn]	n.	结构，布局；配置
portable ['pɔ:təbl]	adj.	轻便的；手提式的
gravity-style	n.	重力式
over-the-road trailers		运行在公路上的拖车

【Notes to Text B】

[1] The type of equipment most used is forklift trucks, walking-rider pallet trucks, towlines, tractor-trailer devices, conveyors and so on.

当使用"such as"时，一般已默认接下来的会是一些不完整的列举，因此不需加上"and so on"或"etc."等。

"such as"是举例，后面加举的例子；"and so on"用在举的例子最后，表示"等等"的意思。

[2] Many types of forklift trucks are available, high-stacking trucks capable of up to 40 feet of vertical movement, pallet less side-clamp versions, and trucks capable of operating in aisles as 56 inches can be found in logistical warehouses.

"be capable of"是固定搭配，表示"有……的能力"，其他介词不与"capable"搭配。

less side-clamp versions 少侧钳位

[3] Towlines consist of either in-floor or overhead-mounted drag devices.

"in-floor"意为"安装在地面的"；"overhead-mounted"意为"安装在空中的"。

consist of 包括；由……组成

[4] Order selectors place merchandise on a four-wheel trailer, which is then towed to the shipping dock.

place on 把……放在……上；把……强加于……；重视；着眼于……

例如:

In conclusion, we must take into account this problem rationally and place more emphases on peasants' lives. 总之，我们应理智考虑这一问题，重视农民的生活。

[5] Portable gravity-style roller conveyors are often used at the warehouse for loading and unloading and, in some cases, are transported on over-the-road trailers to assist in unloading at the destination.

in some cases 在某些情况下

例如:

In some cases the slag can be disposed of usefully. 有时炉渣也有用处。

In some cases, depending on user workflows, tabbed panes can be appropriate. 在某些情况下，根据我们的工作流程，可以使用标签窗格。

This may fail in some cases. 在某些情况下，这样可能会失败。

【Exercises to Text B】

I. True or false.

1. Warehouse can be classified into private warehouse, public warehouse and contract warehouse. ( )
2. Private warehouses are operated by the carriers. ( )
3. Manufacturing firms also utilize public warehouses. ( )
4. When using public warehousing service, it is hard for a firm to change the location and size of inventory. ( )
5. Contract warehouse operators can offer other value-adding activities such as order processing, product inspection. ( )

II. Fill in the blanks.

1. For many years, enterprises had two choices with respect to _____ —public and private.
2. Principal warehousing activities include receipt of products, _____, shipment, and order picking.
3. Private warehouses are usually designed to _____ a variety of items, while private warehouses are more specialized.
4. Most firms depend on a _____ to standardize work procedures and encourage best practice.
5. Every user of warehousing _____ wants it to operate with highest efficiency.
6. Contract warehouse can provide _____ and specially tailored warehousing services.
7. Warehouse emphasizes the storage of product and their _____ purpose is to maximize usage of available storage space.
8. Modern warehouses _____ a wide range of handling equipment.

III. Reading and answering questions.

Increased demand for metal from the Far East, together with speculative investment in base metals by financial investors, has led to record international lead and copper prices, with the prices of others such as aluminum, nickel and zinc following suit. These increased prices have resulted in more incidents of metal theft in the UK.

Spurred on by potentially large rewards, thieves are becoming increasingly bold and their targets more unusual. Many of the thefts are carried out in broad daylight with thieves posing as innocent workmen. Lead, copper and stainless steel roof coverings, iron gates, bronze statues, lead and copper rainwater pipes and even brass door knobs have all been stolen in recent months.

Wherever metals are present, there is an increased risk of theft. Even a small loss can have a significant impact on your business as it takes time to repair damage and source replacement stock or equipment. Further, a business insurance policy does not usually cover as standard theft of either property in the open or of parts of the building.

As long as the value of scrap metal is inflated, metal theft will continue to be a high risk. We therefore recommend that you re-evaluate your premises' existing security arrangements.

There are a number of measures that you can take to deter metal thieves, including:

(1) Remove any easy access to building roofs, water butts, waste bins and trees. Cut back tall trees and vegetation that could provide a screen for criminal activities. Remember to get the necessary approval for any tree cutting before work starts.

(2) Store ladders and any easy means of transporting stolen goods (e.g., wheelie bins and wheelbarrows) in a secure place.

(3) Check roofs regularly. Theft of roofing materials can let rainwater into the building, causing further damage.

(4) Improve the physical security of your premises. Be sure to agree in advance any changes to your intruder alarm protection with your insurer.

(5) If you have stocks of metals, review the existing security arrangements. Many businesses take measures to protect their computer equipment against theft but overlook protection for metals in the workshop or stockyard.

(6) Review perimeter security. Keep any gates locked and restrict vehicular access to the site. Consider retractable bollards over the gated entrance for use out of working hours.

(7) Consider installing security lighting around the building and site, particularly at roof level if there is a metal roof covering.

(8) Consider installing CCTV and display prominent warning notices around the site.

Questions:

1. (   ) has caused the increase in metal price.
   A. increased demand for metals
   B. increased incidents of metal theft
   C. decreased means of transporting metals
   D. deceased investment in metals

2. Prices of (   ) have been increasing.
   A. lead and copper   B. aluminum   C. nickel and zinc   D. all of the above

3. The word "spurred" in Para. 2 means (   ).
   A. stimulated   B. discouraged   C. prevented   D. improved

4. Which of the following is not true according to the passage? (   )
   A. Re-evaluating existing security arrangements can help to prevent metal thieves.
   B. Many thieves pose as innocent workmen and steal metals in broad daylight.
   C. Business insurance policy usually covers loss of metal parts of buildings.
   D. Increased prices of metals caused more incidents of metal theft in the UK.

5. Measures to prevent metal theft include the following except (   ).
    A. cutting back tall trees and vegetation around the stockyard
    B. storing ladders and wheelbarrows in a secure place
    C. taking measures to protect information on metal stocks
    D. restricting vehicular access to the stockyard

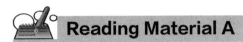

Reading Material A

Web Firms Go on Warehouse Building Boom

The Internet's top retailers aren't **sneering at** giant warehouse anymore—they are building them. This wasn't supposed to happen. Much of the early excitement about **electronic commerce** (e-commerce) involved the belief that companies could serve millions of customers without needing anything approaching the **infrastructure** of a Sears or Walmart. E-commerce companies were supposed to be incredibly efficient **clusters** of computer programmers, who used outside subcontractors to handle such dreary tasks as keeping inventory, filling orders and handling customer-service issues. But now online merchants are discovering that if they don't control their own warehouse and shipping, their reliability ratings with customers can turn dismal. Amazon.com, for example, is in the midst of a US $300 million distribution center initiative that involves building giant facilities in Nevada, Kentucky and Kansas to handle its inventory of books, music, toys and electronics. An online grocery retailer, Webvan Group Inc. has placed a US $1 billion order with Bechtel Group for giant warehouse in 26 cities across the U.S.A.. And other **electronic merchants** such as eToys Inc.and Barnesandnoble.com are pushing ahead with big warehouse projects as well.

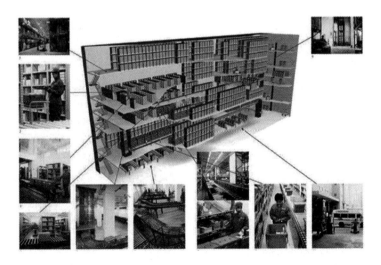

Such investments may be essential if e-commerce companies hope to build up a base of loyal customers, says Steve Johnson, co-director of the e-commerce program at Anderson Consulting. "Customer **acquisition** costs are quite high for these companies, and the only way to get a **pay off** is if you get a lot of repeat business from people," he says, "One bad experience and you have blown it forever." But Internet companies face a steep learning curve as they try to master the shipping and warehouse business. Books and compact disks can be shunted through a warehouse without much trouble, but bulky, odd-size items such as toys and electronics are a lot more difficult. Also, customer return rates can be as high as 30 percent in categories such as apparel, posing big challenges in handling such merchandise. What's more, the make-it-up-as-we-go-along culture of many Internet companies may mesh badly with the logistics industry's need for careful, precise planning. In a recent interview, Webvan's chief executive officer, Lewis Borders, said: "You would laugh at some of our design errors." Heavy equipment targeted for a corner of Webvan's Oakland, California warehouse site had to be relocated after it was discovered that poor soil couldn't support the load, he said.

Some e-commerce companies delegate warehousing and shipping to specialists in that area. But some of the most ambitious internet retailers argue that, for all the additional headaches, it is still worth going into these logistics businesses themselves. "The closer we are to the customers, the more we can build up the lifetime value of our relationships with them," says Jonathan Bulkeley, CEO of Barnesandnoble.com. To oversee these facilities, e-commerce companies are recruiting executives who have plenty of experience in the heavy-lifting end of the business. With some effort, the Internet and logistics cultures are trying to blend together.

【Key Words】

sneer at		嘲笑；讥笑
electronic commerce		电子商务（简写为 e-commerce）
infrastructure ['ɪnfrəstrʌktʃə(r)]	n.	基础设施；基础建设
clusters ['klʌstəz]	n.	群；簇，串（cluster 的复数形式）
	v.	（使）集中（cluster 的第三人称单数形式）
electronic merchant		电商
acquisition [ˌækwɪ'zɪʃn]	n.	收购，获得；购置物
pay off		付清；（付清工资后）解雇

【Questions】

1. Warehouse building are so popular with retailers. Why?
2. How about electronic merchants?
3. What about delegation in that area?

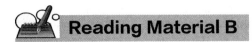

Reading Material B

VMI Technical Implementation Plan

VMI (**Vendor** Managed Inventory) is a kind of cooperation strategy which aims to get the lowest cost for both users and suppliers. Under a common agreement, VMI is managed by suppliers, and constantly monitors the implementation of the agreement and revises the content of the agreement, so that inventory management can be continuously improved.

Next, the implementation process and effect of VMI is introduced by the implementation of the VMI project between P&G and a Hong Kong **retailer**.

The retailer has 10 stores and a distribution center, and manual orders are used before the implementation of the project. VMI technology adopts KARs software + EDI of P&G company.

Before the implementation of the project, P&G's single product number was 115; the central warehouse inventory was 8 weeks; the store inventory was 7 weeks; the out of stock rate was 5%. After analyzing the high inventory and out of stock rate of retailers, the relevant personnel of P&G chose to implement VMI technology to solve the problem of effective **replenishment** of P&G products. The project was officially launched in March 2000. P&G and retail customers invested in the information technology, logistics storage and transportation, **procurement** business departments of both sides, and established a multi-functional team. In the process of several months' implementation, the order, storage and transportation processes were recombined, the standard processes, clear roles and tasks were determined, the VMI system was installed, and the communication channels of electronic data exchange were established.

The system began operation in July 2000. Three months later, the business indicators improved significantly and the economic benefits were significant. Retail sales (P&G products) increased by 40%; P&G commodity single item number increased by 141 (26%); central warehouse inventory decreased by 50% for 4 weeks; store inventory decreased by 17% for 5.8 weeks; shortage rate decreased by 3% (40%). Not only that, the supply chain management of retailers is on a scientific, reasonable and efficient track. All links work in an orderly manner under the new system, which greatly saves the labor intensity of personnel, improves the efficiency and reduces the operation cost.

The implementation of VMI project should pay attention to the following points:

(1) The two sides have good cooperative relationship and trust each other. They are willing to improve supply chain management, improve efficiency and achieve win-win.

(2) The senior management of both sides should pay enough attention to the implementation of relevant responsible personnel, so as to lay a foundation for close cooperation between all departments in the future.

(3) Negotiate reasonable inventory level, transportation cost and other indicators, calculation formula of recommended order.

(4) Close cooperation among information technology, procurement, logistics, storage and transportation departments.

(5) The high accuracy of daily single product sales and inventory data (IRA > 98%) is the basis of VMI.

(6) The store's replenishment is predictable, which can exclude the occasional bulk purchase data.

(7) Business process improvement, optimization and implementation. This is the most difficult and time-consuming item in the project. Because the process of auto replenishment system includes many processes of retailers' daily business and management, and the accuracy of data in each link will affect the accuracy of the final result.

Business process reengineering is the result of close cooperation, precise research and repeated optimization of each department.

From this we can know that, VMI is an inevitable trend in the development of supply chain management. VMI can meet the needs of downstream enterprises to reduce costs and improve service quality. What VMI pursues is a win-win situation. At the same time, it brings many benefits to the suppliers in the upstream of the supply chain. The investment of downstream enterprises is correspondingly reduced. The suppliers are more experienced and professional in product management.

【Key Words】

vendor ['vendə(r)]	n.	卖主；小贩；供应商；自动售货机
retailer ['ri:teilə(r)]	n.	零售商；传播的人
replenishment [ri'pleniʃmənt]	n.	补充，补给
procurement [prə'kjʊrmənt]	n.	采购；获得，取得

【Questions】

1. What is the definition of VMI?
2. What are the advantages and disadvantages of VMI?

Chapter 6
Packaging Management

【参考音频】

IKEA Changed the Packaging of Tea Candle

IKEA was founded in 1943. It has been recognized as one of the world's best retailers in terms of sales volume, growth, number of stores and number of countries. The company has also been recognized as viewing packaging and logistics as important factors for success.

At IKEA stores, the customers select their products directly from the stock that is displayed in the store or immediately receive them from the store warehouse and take them home, where they carry out the final **assembly operation**. IKEA has total control over the supply chain from the supplier to the **end-customer**. Today, there are more than 200 IKEA stores in 31 countries and the range of products is almost the same in every country. The main market is Europe (82%), followed by North America (15%) and Asia (3%). In the beginning IKEA primarily worked with furniture, but now the availability of accessories and **ancillary** products are just as important. This broadened product range has resulted in a number of different packaging solutions, where IKEA had to leave its original "flat package, home assembly" concept.

IKEA's distribution and the packaging solution have from the beginning been set for the European distribution on Euro pallets. This has become a limiting factor as the market has become more global. IKEA decided that the packaging issues had to be addressed. A packaging support function was set up in 1999, called the Packaging Concept. The idea was that the packaging technicians should be located closer to the products and the product development process. This meant that new systems were developed to fulfill IKEA's different needs.

There has been a continuous search in IKEA to reduce the amount of empty space in packaging and vehicles. In 2002 it was found that GLIMMA (the IKEA product name containing a package with tea candles) had more air than any other package. As the GLIMMA product was a massive sale success, it was obvious that a change in packaging would be very beneficial.

The original consumer package held 100 candles in a plastic bag, see Figure 6.1. The bags were packed in large cardboard containers placed on full-size pallets (1,200mm×800mm), offering a display function. The plastic bag was difficult to handle. The floor space utilisation and display functions were not good.

Chapter 6 Packaging Management

Figure 6.1 New packaging solution to the left, old plastic bag to the right

In November 2002, a project was initiated to improve the product, packaging and distribution. The staff chosen had received internal IKEA education and reported directly to the managing director of the IKEA packaging department, who was working with universities to develop the packaging aspects. They formed a team together with the product development people and the suppliers of the candles. The objective was to make the space wasting bags more effective in all parts of the supply chain from supplier to store. In February 2003, they had identified a solution for the total supply chain which was expected to fulfill all the technical properties of the tea candles. In July 2003, four pallets of the **prototype** solution arrived from the supplier in China.

A European pallet in the new German system holds now 360 packs, each holding 100 tea candles, instead of the original 252 packs of 100 candles on the pallet. That reduced the number of Euro pallets used from 59,524 to 41,667 pallets. This reduction lowered the number of trucks needed for the distribution from warehouse to store by 200 trucks each year. It resulted also in lower costs and less environmental impact. It actually produced 21% less CO_2 emissions from **fossil fuel** used in the vehicle journeys each year. The new packaging solution also required less packaging materials in bags and cardboard boxes. These savings meant that it was possible to increase the profit margin, as the price for 100 tea candles is the same as before.

Time has also been saved in the store. The new packaging solution result in easier handling, faster unpacking and better display opportunities. As one pallet takes five minutes to unpack in the store, IKEA calculates with a saving of 186 working days each year in the stores.

【Outline】

The new solution also promotes the commercial requirements better than before, as less cardboard is visible and less floor space is required per 100-pack. This results in more available space for other products to be displayed and sold in the stores.

【Key Words】

assembly operation		装配作业
end-customer	n.	终端客户
ancillary [æn'siləri]	adj.	辅助的；补充的；附加的
	n.	助手；随从
prototype ['prəutətaip]	n.	原型，雏形；最初形态
fossil fuel		化石燃料

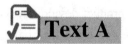

The Importance of Packaging in Logistics

Packing interacts with the logistics system in a number of different and important ways. The size of and protection afforded by the package affect the type of materials-handling equipment used and the level of product damage incurred. The package has an impact on the **stacking** height of the product in the warehouse and thereby on the utilization and cost of the warehouse.[1] Also, from a logistics manager's point of view, packaging is quite important for effective damage protection, not only in the warehouse but also during transportation. Packaging may contribute nothing to a product's value, but its influence on logistics costs is considerable.

Chapter 6　Packaging Management

Package size may affect a company's ability to use **pallets** or shelving or different types of materials-handling equipment. Many companies design packages that are too wide or too high for efficient use of either a warehouse or transportation carrier. So, coordinating packaging with warehousing and with transportation is quite important. Also, poor packaging can contribute to higher handling costs and result in lower future sales if the goods arrived damaged.

Although packaging is important to logistics and supply chain management, it is also of great importance to other functional areas of the company. Like materials handling, packaging **connotes** different things to different people. Since packaging involves a number of organizational areas, these functional entities will need to coordinate their packaging concerns.

Information provision is also important to logistics people. Goods stored in a warehouse must bear the proper identification so that warehouse personnel can locate them easily and correctly.[2] When designing a package, firms may spend a lot of time and effort making sure that it provides information to warehouse personnel. Companies can use **color codes** for placing goods in a ware house. The company should note the weight on the package in order to inform people lifting the package or to determine what can rest on top of it. Techniques for providing information include color coding, universal product codes, **computer-readable tables**, symbols, and **number codes**. A firm's technique or combination of techniques will depend on the organization's particular circumstances.

A major packaging concern is the ease of handling in conjunction with materials handling and transportation. Large packages, for example, may be desirable from a production perspective, but the contents' size and weight might cause problems for materials-handling equipment or for transfer into and out of transportation equipment; so any packaging design should try to maximize **handling ease** in the warehouse and during transportation. Handling ease is also quite important to the production manager, who places the goods in the package.

The important considerations of package design fall into three areas. The first is the package's **physical dimensions**. The design must consider space utilization in terms of the warehouse, transport vehicle, and pallets. The product's physical dimension must also take into account the company's materials-handling equipment. The second consideration is the **package's strength**. The package designer must analyze the package's height, handling, and the type of equipment that will handle the package. The third consideration is package shape.

With customer service playing an ever-increasing role in logistics planning, companies need to integrate their packages with customers' materials-handling equipment.[3] A special package that can interface with a company's innovative equipment may move products inexpensively through its system; however, a customer's **incompatible** equipment will impair its ability to receive and store those goods. In this situation, customer service value may be lost.

A logistics manager's major concern is protecting the goods in the package. In the warehouse, for example, where moving goods could drop from a conveyor or be hit with a forklift truck, the package must provide the product adequate protection. Protection is also important when a transportation agency handles the product. Protection can also mean protecting products from contamination resulting from contact with other goods, water damage, temperature changes, **pilferage**, and shocks in handling and transport. <u>Sometimes packaging must support the weight of products stacked above it, or provide even weight distribution within the package to facilitate manual and automatic materials handling.</u>[4]

【Key Words】

stack [stæk]	v.	堆积；堆起来；覆盖住
	n.	堆，垛；一大堆
package size		包装规格
pallet [ˈpælət]	n.	托盘，货盘；平台；草垫子
connote [kəˈnəut]	vt.	隐含，暗示；意味着
color code		色彩代码
computer-readable table		机读表
number code		数字代码
handling ease		搬运方便
physical dimension		物理维度
package's strength		包装强度
incompatible [ˌinkəmˈpætəbl]	adj.	合不来的，不兼容；不协调的，不相配的
pilferage [ˈpilfəridʒ]	n.	行窃，偷盗

【Notes to Text A】

[1] The package has an impact on the stacking height of the product in the warehouse and thereby on the utilization and cost of the warehouse.

"impact" 在此句中是名词，意为 "影响，作用"。例如：

The computer had made a great impact on modern life. 计算机对现代生活产生了巨大的影响。

"stacking" 是现在分词，作 "height" 的定语。

[2] Goods stored in a warehouse must bear the proper identification so that warehouse personnel can locate them easily and correctly.

"stored in a warehouse" 是过去分词短语作 "goods" 的后置定语。

"personnel" 意为 "人员，员工"。例如：

The personnel are not happy to change these rules. 全体工作人员对改变这些规定很不高兴。

[3] With customer service playing an ever-increasing role in logistics planning, companies need to integrate their packages with customers' materials-handling equipment.

"with customer service playing an ever-increasing role in logistics planning" 是介宾结构，作状语。

"materials-handling" 意为 "物料搬运"。例如：

The materials-handling equipment selection decision is examined from a design perspective, as well as from a pragmatic viewpoint of the factors utilized in the selection decision. 物料搬运设备的选择决策不仅要从实用因素注重实效的观点来看，而且要从设计的角度来检验。

[4] Sometimes packaging must support the weight of products stacked above it, or provide even weight distribution within the package to facilitate manual and automatic materials handling.

"distribution"意为"散布，分布"。例如：

The town council passed a law forbidding the distribution of handbills. 镇议会通过了一项禁止散发传单的法律。

"stacked above it"是过去分词短语作后置定语修饰"products"，相当于从句"which are stacked above it"。

【Exercises to Text A】

I. Translation.

1. We generally discuss two types of packaging: consumer packaging（消费者包装）, or interior packaging（内部包装）; and industrial packaging（工业包装）, or exterior packaging（外部包装）. The marketing manager is usually most concerned about the former because consumer or interior packaging provides information important in selling the product, in motivating the customer to buy the product, or in giving the product maximum visibility when it competes with others on the retail shelf.

2. Hewlett-Packard（惠普公司）ships computer printers from the United States to Europe using airfreight and minimal packaging（精简包装）. They shrink-wrap（收缩包装）unit loads of printers to provide stability and reduce damage. In addition to lowering transportation cost, the overall practice reduces import duties since substantial value-added is postponed until the product is finally assembled and sold in Europe.

3. However, the plastic materials（塑料材料）companies use to cushion the product（衬垫产品）inside the box have possibly done the most to revolutionize packaging. These materials enable manufacturers to highly automate the packaging area and to maximize protection while minimizing costs.

II. Fill in the blanks.

1. The size of and protection _____ by the package affect the type of materials-handling equipment used and the level of product damage incurred.

2. Many companies design packages that are too wide or too high for _____ use of either a warehouse or transportation carrier.

3. Since packaging involves a number of organizational areas, these functional entities will need to their packaging concerns.

4. Companies can use _____ for placing goods in a warehouse.

5. The important considerations of package design fall into three areas. The first is the package's _____.

6. Changes in federal and state regulation have also affected packaging's protection aspect, especially in food and drug product areas, where companies must design packaging to reduce consumer anxieties about _____.

Text B

Packaging Helps to Optimize Logistics Units

1. Greater Efficiency with Intelligent Consolidation

With the help of packaging, logistics units like the Euro pallet can be created in order to transport products as collective units. Ideally, these units remain intact throughout the delivery chain and do not have to be broken down into their components.[1] The **optimal** situation for a logistics manager would be to pack a number of just-finished goods onto a pallet, load it along with other units onto a tractor-trailer rig and then deliver the entire load to the customer. Loading, transshipping and unloading of logistics units could be easily done by such **auxiliary** devices as forklifts.

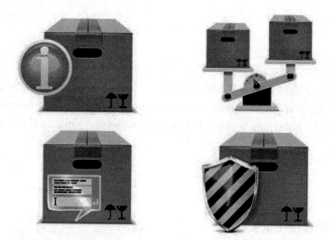

2. Streamlining the Transport Chain

Logistics units result from the **consolidation** of goods in units of standardized form and dimension.[2] The aim is to simplify the flow of goods and thereby lower costs. The procedure is

Chapter 6　Packaging Management

aptly called "unitization". The basic idea behind the concept is this: the fewer components in the flow of a given amount of goods from the supplier to the customer, the more smoothly it can be carried out.

The logistics unit plays a central role in the entire logistics system since it represents the link between the individual phases of the flow of goods. The formation of logistics units is therefore a condition for an efficient transport chain.

The transport chain can be streamlined by:

(1) Grouping goods into larger units.

(2) Standardizing the units' form and size.

(3) Facilitating the use of mechanical devices during handling operations.

(4) Ensuring unit stackability.

(5) Selecting a unit that enables a largely continuous transport chain from the supplier to the customer.

3. The Variety of Logistics Units

Logistics units come in all forms. These include large and small containers as well as box, flat and stack pallets. The following section provides detailed descriptions about these optimal logistics units.

Large Containers

Small Containers

Box Pallet

Flat Pallet

(1) Large containers.

Large containers include sea containers or ISO containers that are used to perform much of international trade. The ubiquitous ISO containers are 8 feet wide (2.438m) and are either 20 feet (6.096m) or 40 feet (12.192m) long. The term TEU is the standard worldwide measure for a container. A TEU is a 20-foot-long container. A 40-foot container amounts to two TEUs.

The American Malcolm McLean was the person who came up with the idea of using standard containers for sea transport. With his invention of the sea container he revolutionized international trade or even made it universally possible, contributing considerably to globalization.

Another example of large containers is air-freight containers, **so-called** ULD (unit load device) containers. ULD containers are made of lightweight material such as aluminum. Different standard dimensions are suited for different types of aircraft. They are designed to exactly fit the **interior** of the respective aircraft, ensuring that the plane's precious **cargo hold** can be optimally used. The strength of these containers is that fewer units have to be loaded, generating savings in time, expense and ground personnel.

(2) Small containers.

Small containers are suited for small parts being stored, picked or transported within a business operation. They have standard sizes and can often be stacked, a feature that enables several small containers to be packed collectively into a logistics unit on pallets.[3] Small containers include plastic containers, cardboard boxes, foldable units, insulated cases and special containers for foods or bulk cargo.

(3) Box pallet.

The box pallet is a combination of container and pallet. It is based on a pallet and has a **superstructure** of wire mesh, sheet metal or wood. It is used to store an assortment of packaged goods in large quantities or with large volumes.

(4) Flat pallet.

The best known flat pallet in Europe is the Euro pallet. It is a load-bearer that has been normed by European transport companies. Pallets of 800 mm × 1,200 mm are widely used in Europe. Several other ISO standard sizes have also been defined for pallets. In North America, pallets measuring 48 inches by 40 inches, or 1,219 mm × 1,016 mm, are most often used. As a rule, Euro pallets are not used in ISO containers because the Euro pallet does not fit into the ISO container. The reason for the different sizes lies in the systems' **disparate** origins. The ISO container was developed in the United States, the Euro pallet in Europe.

(5) Stack pallet.

The stack pallet is a flat pallet with four corner columns that facilitate the stacking of pallets on top of one another.[4] The vertical columns on the four corners of the pallet have a standard profile and are either fixed or removable. The external dimensions and the carrying capacity of the stack pallet are roughly those of the box pallet. When several of these structures are stacked vertically, stack pallets can also be used as pallet racks.

【Key Words】

optimal ['ɔptiməl]	adj.	最佳的，最优的；最理想的
auxiliary [ɔːgˈziliəri]	adj.	辅助的；备用的；附加的
	n.	助动词；辅助人员；附属机构
consolidation [kənˌsɔliˈdeiʃən]	n.	巩固；合并
aptly ['æptli]	adv.	适当地；巧妙地
so-called	adj.	所谓的；号称的
interior [inˈtiəriə(r)]	n.	内部；内地；内政；内心
	adj.	内部的；内地的；国内的；内心的
cargo hold		货舱

superstructure [ˈsuːpəstrʌktʃər]   *n.* 上部结构，上层建筑；（建筑物、船等的）上面部分
disparate [ˈdɪspərət]   *adj.* 完全不同的

【Notes to Text B】

[1] Ideally, these units remain intact throughout the delivery chain and do not have to be broken down into their components.

"intact" 意为 "完整无缺的，未经触动的"。例如：
He can scarcely survive this scandal with his reputation intact. 他经此丑闻后，名誉很难不受损。
"break down into" 意为 "分成不同种类；分解成……"。例如：
Physically, the rocks break down into smaller and smaller pieces. 物理上，岩石会分解成越来越小的碎片。

[2] Logistics units result from the consolidation of goods in units of standardized form and dimension.

"result from" 意为 "产生于……，由……引起"。例如：
His failure resulted from not working hard enough. 他的失败是工作不够努力造成的。
"consolidation" 意为 "巩固；联合；合并；变坚固"。例如：
Even if not total, the Romans' hold was sufficient for them to begin the task of consolidation. 即使没有实现完全的控制，罗马人的势力也足以让他们着手巩固政权了。

[3] They have standard sizes and can often be stacked, a feature that enables several small containers to be packed collectively into a logistics unit on pallets.

"a feature" 指的是 "they have standard sizes and can often be stacked"，它们是同位语。
"collectively" 意为 "全体地，共同地"。例如：
In 1968 the states collectively spent US $2 billion on it. 1968 年，各州在这上面总共花费了 20 亿美元。

[4] The stack pallet is a flat pallet with four corner columns that facilitate the stacking of pallets on top of one another.

"facilitate" 意为 "促进，使容易；帮助"。例如：
The new airport will facilitate the development of tourism. 新机场将促进旅游业的发展。
"with four corner columns" 是介词短语，修饰 "pallet"；"that facilitate the stacking of pallets on top of one another" 是定语从句，修饰 "columns"。

【Exercises to Text B】

I. Answer the following questions.

1. What is the feature of ideal logistics units?
2. What is the basic idea of "unitization"?
3. How can you streamline the transport chain?
4. What are the 5 primary logistics units?

II. Fill in the blanks.

disparate   superstructure   interior   so-called   aptly   consolidation   auxiliary   optimal

1. The _____ flatlands and valleys are thickly planted with coconuts.
2. The state ensures the _____ and growth of the state economy.
3. This word is _____ used here.
4. The _____ systems differ according to the criterion chosen.
5. Chalk and cheese are _____ substances.
6. More and more companies have gone "green" and started producing _____ environmentally-friendly products.
7. The system includes a backup _____ system.
8. With the change of the economic foundation the entire immense _____ is more or less rapidly transformed.

Reading Material

Green Packaging Management of Logistics Enterprises

Green packaging, which can also be called "**ecological packaging**" or "environmentally friendly packaging", is defined as environmental friendly package, which is completely made by natural plants, can be circle or secondly used, be prone to degradation and promote sustainable development. During its whole lifecycle, green packaging is harmless to environment as well as to human body and livestock's health. In short, green packaging is the appropriate packaging that can be reused, recycled or degradation, corruption and does not cause pollution in humans and the environment during the product life cycle.

Green packaging is not only a package of general performance, but also with two main functions such as protecting the environment and renewing resources. The two main functions are achieved by the principles of 4R1D, short for Reduce, Reuse, Reclaim, Recycle and Degradable.

Reduce, that is packaging reduction. On the premise that packaging meets the needs of protection, facilitating logistics and sales, logistics enterprises should try to use as little material as possible. European and American countries have developed packaging reduction as the preferred measures of package. In order to implement the measure of appropriate amount of packaging, companies should design and try to make the package thin, lightweight.

Reuse, that is repeated use of packaging. After simple treatment, the containers can be reused. Reuse of containers can significantly reduce waste volume. To use reusable containers as much as possible will enhance recycling rate of packaging waste reuse.

Reclaim, also called recyclable. Refers to the use of packaging waste **combustion** to obtain new energy sources, and does not produce secondary pollution. Through the recycling of packaging waste, production of renewable products, such as the use of thermal **incineration**, composting and other measures to improve the land condition, to achieve reuse purposes.

Recycle, means to treat packaging that have already been used so that they can be used

Chapter 6   Packaging Management

again. As far as possible to use low power consumption, low-cost, low-pollution raw materials as packaging material, in particular, the selection of recycled materials should be expanded, which can not only reduce environmental pollution but also saves raw materials, and be **propitious** to recycling resources, such as production of recycled paper board and plastic.

Degradable, means the ultimate packaging waste that cannot be reused of, should be able to degrade, corrupt and do not form a permanent waste. For example, select biodegradable packaging materials of paper as more as possible. "Take paper on the plastic's place."

For enterprises, the development of green logistics is the trend. Logistics managers should assess the situation and actively respond to shorten the gap of the green logistics operations, and make a further green recycling of logistics processes. Six green packaging management strategies can be adopted.

(1) Using green packaging materials. Green packaging materials are the recycled materials causing the minimum of burden to the environment and maximum **coefficient** of utilization in the whole process of the life cycle. Green packaging material is the core of green packaging, which not only reduce and eliminate the environment pollution, **alleviate** the pressure on the ecological environment, but also conserve or replace some of the expensive or lack resources in order to reuse waste resources. Based On sustainable development strategy, environmental performance must be as an important aspect to study when choosing packaging materials. The strategy of sustainable development must proceeded from, considering the material's three elements, performance, economy and environment (including resources, energy, environmental protection). Using green packaging materials is the fundamental way to ensure the sustainable development strategy angle from the material.

(2) Lowering costs of packaging. The largest proportion of packaging cost is the packaging material cost, so lower costs should start from reducing packaging material cost. So organizations need reasonable packaging materials procurement, under the premise of ensuring the basic functions, to minimize the grade of material. Using common packing that does not have special arrangements for the return of the use. **Turnover packaging** can be used repeatedly, such as drinks, beer bottles; Repetition utilization is that the packaging turn to another material after the first use by a simple treatment. Using simplified packaging and reach appropriate packaging. Packaging reduction, to reduce packaging waste from source, is world idly recognized as the preferred means of packaging green. The formation of excessive packaging waste is also a cause unnecessary pollution.

(3) Making package unit large-scale and containerized. Large-scale packaging of logistics system **conducive** to mechanization process in handling, removal, storage and transportation, and speed up the operating speed of these links; It helps to reduce the unit packaging, and to save packaging materials and packaging cost; It also helps to protect the cargo body, such as the use of container bags, containers, pallets and other container means.

(4) Developing new packaging materials and packaging equipment. To develop packaging

materials of lightweight, thin, conducive, high performance is an important direction of the green packaging materials. On the basis of guarantee the implementation of the three big functions, we should reform excessive packaging and develop proper packaging, as well as try to cut down the use of wrapping and packaging costs and save the packaging material resources.

(5) Minimizing the type of material that used. In order to simplify the manufacturing process of the packaging, and make packaging more easy on **disassembly** and recycling, sorting and recycling, packaging design should try to avoid using many different types of materials and should be designed easily separated by the structural for the complex packaging.

(6) Putting green packaging signs in practice. Under the concept of green consumption, people not only concern about the quality of the goods and weather packaging is beautiful, but also care about if the product compliance with environmental requirements and if the packaging has a green flag in the purchase of goods. Also, if products do not have green flag, some developed countries refused to import them, and do not give preferential price and tax. Therefore, the development of greenl ogistics is a powerful symbol and one of the necessary ways for the enterprise to extend towards the world.

【Key Words】

ecological packaging		生态包装
combustion [kəmˈbʌstʃən]	n.	燃烧，烧毁；氧化
incineration [inˌsinəˈreiʃn]	n.	焚化；火葬
propitious [prəˈpiʃəs]	adj.	有利的；吉祥的；合适的
coefficient [ˌkəuiˈfiʃnt]	n.	系数；程度；协同因素
alleviate [əˈliːvieit]	vt.	减轻，缓解
turnover packaging		周转包装
conducive [kənˈdjuːsiv]	adj.	有助于……的；有益于……的
disassembly [ˌdisəˈsembli]	n.	拆卸，分解；解体；拆开

【Questions】

1. What are green packaging's principles of 4R1D?
2. What strategies can be adopted to promote the application of green packaging?

Chapter 7
Distribution Management

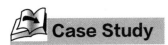

【参考音频】

Distribution Management:
Control and Collaboration from Supplier to Customer

Your distribution network extends from your supplier's loading dock to your customer's front door—far beyond the walls of your warehouse. Save a step or simplify a process, and you deliver faster—which not only **enhances** your bottom line, but also improves service levels. When you're dealing with scores of suppliers on distant continents, 3PL companies, **multiple** distribution centers and customers around in the world, getting visibility into the full distribution process can be extremely challenging.

Manhattan Associates' Distribution Management is a complete suite of solutions to automate every link in the most complex supply chains. Distribution Management is anchored by Manhattan's proven and industry-leading warehouse management solutions. It is engineered for optimal collaboration and communication with an extensive network of suppliers and partners—but does not require any of them to make a major technology investment to do business with you.

With confidence in your ability to work closely with your network, suppliers and customers, you can fill orders even before you have received the product. You will have the information you need to motivate your suppliers, as well as your own workforce, to move products faster and more accurately—for happier customers and less happy competitors.

Distribution Management spans your supply chain network with this extensive suite of products:

(1) Warehouse Management—Fine-tune your facility with a more efficient layout, well utilized resources, streamlined inventory and flawless order fulfillment.

(2) Slotting Optimization—Match slots to demand, weight and other product characteristics for faster, more accurate picking resulting in improved productivity.

(3) Labor Management—Standardize and track workforce performance throughout your operation. Reward quality and safety, boost productivity and forecast with better precision.

(4) Labor Scheduling Optimization—Automate workforce planning and scheduling to lower unit labor costs, **maximize** skill sets, and increase customer service and productivity.

(5) Billing Management—Assign and manage charges for virtually any warehouse event for a full understanding of your costs and profits. Track activities by unit or client.

(6) Supplier Enablement—Extend powerful supply chain capabilities to your suppliers, and automate communications and record-keeping—all online.

(7) Hub Management—Give hubs and 3PL providers instant visibility of orders, shipments and inventory. Streamline transport and inventory by managing partner-to-partner shipping.

Chapter 7 Distribution Management

【Key Words】

enhance [in'hɑːns]	vt.	提高，增加；改进
multiple ['mʌltipl]	adj.	多重的；多个的；多功能的
	n.	倍数；并联；连锁商店
maximize ['mæksimaiz]	vt.	最大化；使增至最大限度；最大限度地利用（某事物）
	vi.	尽可能广义地解释；达到最大值

Text A

Concept of Distribution Management

1. Definition for Distribution Management

The business for distribution management is that the management of the efficient transfer of goods from the **place of manufacture** to the **point of sale** or consumption. Distribution management encompasses such activities as warehousing, materials handling, packaging, stock control, order processing, and transportation, etc..

2. The Importance of Distribution Management

Distribution management is an integral part of company management, which is a **crucial** concern for businesses that operate in global markets **transformed** by new information and communication technologies.[1] Products and services are increasingly developed, produced, and sold in different geographic regions. Companies **outsource** as many non-core activities to other firms around the world as possible. Thus, transportation and distribution networks may influence **performance** and competitiveness within international markets.

3. The Function of Distribution Management

The distribution management consists of four **subordinate** organization units: the sales management, product delivery, transport management and vehicle management divisions.[2] **Compendiously**, the distribution management handles customer orders, generates sales plans, and ships products to customers. The sales management is responsible for managing orders and contracts, generating sales and delivery plans, and making statistics of sales and settlement data. The transport management is responsible for arranging sufficient transport capacities, making timetables of loading and dispatching. The product delivery is responsible for loading the goods and measuring the product **fluxes**, in accordance with the bills of lading. The vehicle management division is responsible for managing the vehicle owned by the company.

4. Distribution Management System

A distribution management system performs a wide range of information **transactions**, such as customer order entry, distribution planning, transport arrangement, vehicle scheduling, product loading, measuring control, issuing entry/exit **visas**, generating statistical reports of sales, etc..

5. Function View Model

Function view models (see Figure 7.1) are created to **represent** the functional relationships among the information processing transactions:[3]

(1) Sales Management is responsible for generating sales plans, handling customer orders, and providing foundations for finance settlements.

(2) Transport Management is responsible for arranging transport capacities, **itineraries** and timetables for carrying out product deliveries.[4] A fundamental issue of the transport management in a company is to arrange sufficient vehicle and **optimally** schedule them against tracks.

(3) Delivery Management generates **log files** on vehicle entries(exits), carries out the loading orders and controls the loading processes.

(4) Vehicle Management records and provides status information of the vehicle owned by the company. It is also responsible for routine maintenance of the vehicle.

Chapter 7 Distribution Management

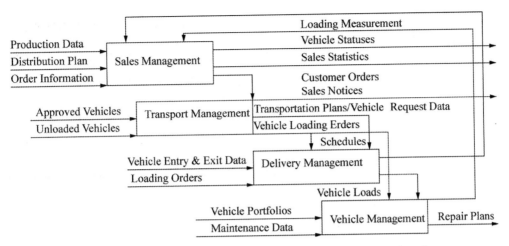

Figure 7.1 Function view model of the distribution management system

【Key Words】

place of manufacture		生产地点
point of sale		销售地点
crucial ['kru:ʃl]	adj.	关键的；至关重要的
transform [træns'fɔ:m]	vt.	使改变形态，使改观
outsource ['autsɔ:s]	vt.	外包（工程）；外购
performance [pə'fɔ:məns]	n.	演出，演奏；履行，完成；成绩；性能
	adj	性能卓越的
subordinate [sə'bɔ:dənit]	adj.	下级的（+to）；次要的，隶属的（+to）
compendiously [kəm'pendiəsli]	adv.	简洁地；扼要地
flux [flʌks]	n.	流动；波动；变迁
transaction [træn'zækʃn]	n.	办理，处置；执行；交易，业务
visa ['vi:zə]	n.	签证
represent [ˌrepri'zent]	vt.	描绘；代表；象征
itinerary [ai'tinərəri]	n.	旅程，路线；旅行计划；旅行指南
optimally ['ɔptiməli]	adv.	最佳地
log files		日志文件

【Notes to Text A】

[1] Distribution management is an integral part of company management, which is a crucial concern for businesses that operate in global markets transformed by new information and communication technologies.

"that operate in global markets transformed by new information and communication technologies"是"that"引导的定语从句,修饰"businesses"。

[2] The distribution management consists of four subordinate organization units: the sales management, product delivery, transport management and vehicle management divisions.

"consists of"是动词短语,意为"由……组成/构成"。

[3] Function view models are created to represent the functional relationships among the information processing transactions.

"are created to"是被动语态,意为"被用作……"。

[4] Transport Management is responsible for arranging transport capacities, itineraries and timetables for carrying out product deliveries.

"is responsible for"意为"对……负责"。

【Exercises to Text A】

I. Fill in the blanks.

d_____ management
配送管理

place of m_____
生产地点

m_____ handling
物料搬移

non-c_____ activity
非核心活动

product d_____
产品交付

vehicle p_____
车辆组合

point of c_____
消费地点

c_____ concern
关键问题

s_____ organization
下属机构

l_____ files
日志文件

II. Fill in the blanks with proper words or expressions.

1. Companies _____ as many non-core activities to other firms around the world as possible.

2. Transportation and _____ networks may influence _____ and competitiveness within international markets.

3. _____, the distribution management handles customer orders, generates sales plans, and ships products to customers.

4. Delivery management generates _____ on vehicle entries(exits), carries out the loading orders and controls the loading processes.

5. Vehicle management is also responsible for _____ of the vehicle.

III. Please write a paragraph introducing the functional relationships among the information processing transactions of the distribution management system.

IV. Questions for discussion.

1. What is distribution management?
2. Why is the distribution management important for a company?
3. Please describe the function of distribution management.

V. Translation.

1. 配送管理是公司管理必不可少的一部分。

2. 运输和配送网络可能会影响（公司）在国际市场的业绩和竞争力。

3. 配送管理包括单位销售管理、产品交付、运输管理和车辆管理 4 个下属部门。

4. 配送管理系统执行广泛的信息处理。

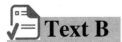 **Text B**

Public and Private Warehouses

A common distinction among warehouses is whether they are public or private. **Distribution** centers can be either, although they emphasize distributing rather than storing goods.

1. Public Warehouses

Public warehouses are **analogous** to common carriers in that they serve all **legitimate** users. Also similar to the common carriers, they have certain responsibilities to their users.

Public warehouses are used by firms that either cannot **justify** the costs of having their own facilities, or prefer not making a **commitment** to owning and operating their own facilities. In most analyses of a firm's warehousing needs, public warehouses are considered as the **initial** alternative. They offer more in the way of flexibility in terms of both space needs and location than would be offered by any system of company-owned facilities. They require no capital investment, and space is rented as needed.

Some public warehouses are specialized. They may handle only refrigerated goods, steel, or household goods, or even be grain **elevators**. **Maritime** general cargo "transit sheds" in ports perform some public warehouse functions, although they are **oriented** more toward moving cargo through than they are to storage.

Many examples could be **cited** of a public warehouseman's functioning as an integral link in a product **distribution channel**. In a city with ten dealers for one make of electrical appliance, none of the **dealers** might stock an inventory. The only models they possess are on their showroom floors. Once they make a sale, they notify the public warehouse, which delivers a unit directly to the buyer's **residence** from the warehouse stock. The warehouse notifies the factory of the sale, and the factory replenishes the warehouse's stock. In this instance, the stock in the inventory in the warehouse belongs to the manufacturer, a factory **distributor**, or an area-wide dealer. Warehouse performs functions that would otherwise have to be performed by the owner of the inventory; the **principal** advantage is that dealers do not have to **maintain** large inventories.[1]

Public warehouses also serve as integral links for other logistical functions. Public warehouses are used by the auto industry; they feed components to the assembly plants on a daily and, sometimes, an hourly basis. With the growing interest in JIT inventory/production systems, there has been some concern as to what role, if any, the public warehouse might play. To a certain extent, the manufacturer may reduce inventories of **inbound** materials on hand by accepting smaller, more frequent deliveries from stocks the **vendor** maintains—often in nearby public warehouses. This shift in responsibility for holding the inventory would result in little net savings unless the vendor were able to do a better job of managing the inventory in warehouses than the user could in the factory. However, the responsibility for inventory has been pushed back one step in the production/supply process. The more this can happen, the better, because each step back toward the **original** source represents a delay in the final user's having to pay certain costs.

2. Private Warehouses

Private warehouses are owned or occupied on a long-term lease by the firm using them. They are used by firms who find that their warehouse needs are so stable that they can make long-term commitments to fixed facilities (Private warehouse operation also requires commitment to a warehouse labor force). The largest users of private warehouses are retail chain stores. They handle large volumes of merchandise on a regular basis, and one of their resulting economies of **scale** comes from integrating the warehousing function with purchasing and distribution to retail **outlets**.

Manufacturing firms also maintain their own warehouses. For a firm manufacturing related products at different locations, each plant ships its items to the firm's **regional** distribution warehouses so that each of them can stock a complete line of products.[2] There are also products with unique handling characteristics such as steel beams or gasoline, that, in some areas, public warehousemen prefer not to handle. In these **circumstance** the manufacturer is forced to develop his own facilities. Contract warehousing refers to long-term **contractual** arrangements for warehouse space and services that combine aspects of both public and private warehouse practices.

3. Plant Warehouses

A warehouse associated with most manufacturing operations is the plant warehouse, usually located somewhere near the end of the assembly line.[3] Its principal function is to **accommodate** the differences in production line **output** and product demand in the distribution network. The plant warehouse may also be the single location where every line item in the firm's inventory is stocked.

4. Distribution Center

The phrase distribution center is applied somewhat loosely. Some public warehouses refer to themselves as distribution centers, which they emphasize the distribution aspects of warehousing instead of the storage operations. The emphasis is on fast **turn-over** of goods.

【Key Words】

distinction [dɪˈstɪŋkʃn]	n.	差别，分别；卓越；荣誉
public warehouses		公共仓库
analogous [əˈnæləgəs]	adj.	相似的，可比拟的
legitimate [lɪˈdʒɪtɪmət]	adj.	合法的，合理的；正规的；真实的
justify [ˈdʒʌstɪfaɪ]	vt.	证明……有理；对……作出解释
	vi.	整理版面；证明合法
commitment [kəˈmɪtmənt]	n.	信奉，忠诚；承诺；投入，花费
initial [ɪˈnɪʃl]	adj.	开始的
	n.	首字母
elevatory [ˈelɪveɪtəri]	adj.	向上举的，升高的
maritime [ˈmærɪtaɪm]	adj.	海上的，海事的，海运的
oriented [ˈɔːrientɪd]	adj.	对……感兴趣的；以……为方向的
cite [saɪt]	v.	引用；引证
distribution channel		配送渠道
dealer [ˈdiːlə(r)]	n.	经销商，商人
residence [ˈrezɪdəns]	n.	住处，住宅；居住时间，居住；驻地
distributor [dɪˈstrɪbjətə(r)]	n.	批发公司，批发商；分发者，分配者
principal [ˈprɪnsəpl]	n.	负责人，首长，校长，本金
	adj.	主要的，首要的

maintain [meɪnˈteɪn]	vt.	维持，维修；继续，供养
inbound [ˈɪnbaʊnd]	adj.	本地的，本土的；归航的
vendor [ˈvendə(r)]	n.	卖主
original [əˈrɪdʒənl]	adj.	最初的，原始的；独创的，新颖的
	n.	原物，原作
private warehouses		私有仓库
scale [skeɪl]	n.	刻度，衡量，比例，数值范围，等级
	v.	测量，衡量
outlet [ˈaʊtlet]	n.	出口；销路；批发商店
regional [ˈriːdʒənl]	adj.	整个地区的，地方地，地域性地
circumstance [ˈsɜːkəmstəns]	n.	环境，详情，境况
contractual [kənˈtræktʃuəl]	adj.	契约的
accommodate [əˈkɒmədeɪt]	vt.	供应，供给；使适应；调节，和解
	vi.	适应
output [ˈaʊtpʊt]	n.	输出，生产量；产品；生产
turn-over	n.	营业额；周转率

【Notes to Text B】

[1] Warehouse performs functions that would otherwise have to be performed by the owner of the inventory; the principal advantage is that dealers do not have to maintain large inventories.

"dealer" 意为"销售商，经销商"，后者用得多些。

[2] For a firm manufacturing related products at different locations, each plant ships its items to the firm's regional distribution warehouses so that each of them can stock a complete line of products.

其中，"products at different locations" 意为"生产于异地的零部件产品"。"ship" 意为"装上船，载运"，此处译成"载运"较好。

此处 "items" 可理解为"各地工厂提供的不同产品"。

[3] A warehouse associated with most manufacturing operations is the plant warehouse, usually located somewhere near the end of the assembly line.

其中，"the assembly line" 意为"装配线"。

【Exercises to Text B】

I. Fill in the blanks.

1. _____ are analogous to common carriers in that they serve all legitimate users.

2. The warehouse principal advantage is that dealers _____ have to maintain large inventories.

3. _____ are owned or occupied on a long-term lease by the firm using them.

4. _____ 's principal function is to accommodate the differences in production line output and product demand in the distribution network.

5. Some public warehouses refer to themselves as _____.

Chapter 7 Distribution Management

II. True or false.

1. Public warehouses are used by firms that can justify the costs of having their own facilities, or prefer making a commitment to owning and operating their own facilities.   (   )
2. All public warehouses are specialized.   (   )
3. Public warehouses serve as integral links for other logistical functions.   (   )
4. The largest users of private warehouses are not retail chain stores.   (   )
5. Manufacturing firms can maintain their own warehouses.   (   )
6. The plant warehouse may not be the single location where every line item in the firm's inventory is stocked.   (   )

III. Translation.

1. 在大多数仓库需求分析中，公共仓库被认为是首选。

2. 它们不需要资金投入，需要空间时只管去租赁即可。

3. 在这种情况下，仓库里存货属于制造厂商、制造厂批发商或大区经销商。

4. 与大部分生产运作相关的储存是工厂仓库，通常位于装配线（the assembly line）的附近。

5. 要强调的是货物的快速周转。

Text C

Physical Distribution

1. Conception of Physical Distribution

Physical distribution operations involve processing and delivering customer orders. Physical distribution is integral to marketing and sales performance because it provides timely and economical product availability.[1] The overall process of gaining and maintaining customers can be broadly divided into transaction-creation and **physical-fulfillment** activities.[2] The transaction-creating activities are advertising and selling. Physical distribution performs the physical-fulfillment activities.

2. Distribution Performance Cycle

The physical distribution performance cycle involves five related activities. They are order transmission, order processing, order selection, order transportation, and customer delivery. The basic physical distribution performance cycle is **illustrated** in Figure 7.2.

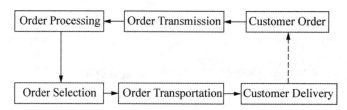

Figure 7.2 The basic distribution performance cycle

From a logistical perspective, physical distribution links a firm with its customers. Physical distribution resolves marketing and manufacturing initiatives into an integrated effort. The interface between marketing and manufacturing can be **conflictive**. On the one hand, marketing is dedicated to delighting customers. In most firms, minimal limits are imposed by marketing and sales when it comes to accommodation customers. Often, this means that marketing and sales would like to maintain a broad product line with high inventory regardless of each product's actual profit potential.[3] In this way, any customer's requirement, no matter how small or large, would be satisfied. The expectation is that zero defect service will be achieved and customer-focused marketing efforts will be supported.

The very fact that physical distribution deals with customer requirements means that related operations will be more **erratic** than characteristic of manufacturing support and procurement performance cycles. Attention to how customers order products is essential to reduce physical distribution operational variance and simplify transactions.[4] First, every effort should be made to improve forecast accuracy. Second, a program of order management coordination with customers should be initiated to reduce uncertainty as much as possible. Third, and finally, physical distribution performance cycles should be designed to be as flexible and responsive as possible.

The key to understanding physical distribution performance-cycle **dynamics** is to keep in mind that customers initiate the process by ordering. The logistical response capability of the selling enterprise constitutes one of the most significant competencies in overall marketing strategy.

3. Types of Distribution

Three types of distribution can be used to make product available to consumers: intensive distribution, selective distribution, and exclusive distribution.

(1) Intensive Distribution.

In intensive distribution, the product is sold to as many appropriate retailers or wholesalers as possible. Intensive distribution is appropriate for products such as chewing gum, candy bar, soft drinks, bread, film, and cigarettes where the primary factor influencing the purchase decision is convenience. Industrial products that may require intensive distribution include pencils, paper clips, **transparent** tape, file folders, typing paper, screws and nails.

(2) Selective Distribution.

In selective distribution, on the other hand, the number of outlets that may carry a product is limited, but not to the extent of exclusive dealing. By carefully selecting wholesalers or retailers, the manufacturer can concentrate on potentially profitable accounts and develop solid working relationships to ensure that the product is properly merchandised. The producer also may restrict the number of retail outlets if the product requires specialized servicing or sales support. Selective distribution may be used for product categories such as clothing, appliances, televisions, stereo equipment, home furnishings, and sports equipment.

(3) Exclusive Distribution.

When a single outlet is given an exclusive **franchise** to sell the product in a geographic area, the arrangement is referred to as exclusive distribution. Products such as specialty automobiles, some major appliances, certain brand of furniture, and lines of clothing that enjoy a high degree of brand loyalty are likely to be distributed on an exclusive basis. This is particularly true if the consumer is willing to overcome the inconvenience of traveling some distance to obtain the product. Usually, exclusive distribution is undertaken when the manufacturer desires more aggressive selling on the part of the wholesaler or retailer, or when channel control is important. Exclusive distribution may enhance the product's image and enable the firm to charge higher retail prices.

【Key Words】

physical distribution		实物配送
physical-fulfillment	n.	实际履行
illustrate ['iləstreit]	v.	解释，说明；加插图于……

conflictive [kən'fliktiv]	adj.	矛盾的，抵触的
erratic [i'rætik]	adj.	不规则的；不稳定的；行为古怪的
dynamics [dai'næmiks]	n.	相互作用；动态；驱动力
transparent [træns'pærənt]	adj.	透明的；易懂的
franchise ['fræntʃaiz]	n.	特许（经营）权；经销权

【Notes to Text C】

[1] Physical distribution is integral to marketing and sales performance because it provides timely and economical product availability.

"because it provides timely and economical product availability" 是 "because" 引导的状语从句。

[2] The overall process of gaining and maintaining customers can be broadly divided into transaction-creation and physical-fulfillment activities.

"transaction-creation and physical-fulfillment" 这种结构为复合词，作形容词修饰 "activities"。

[3] Often, this means that marketing and sales would like to maintain a broad product line with high inventory regardless of each product's actual profit potential.

regardless of 不管，不顾

[4] Attention to how customers order products is essential to reduce physical distribution operational variance and simplify transactions.

"attention to how customers order products" 是主句的主语。

【Exercises to Text C】

I. Fill in the blanks.

1. The overall process of _____ customers can be broadly divided into _____ and physical-fulfillment activities.

2. They are order transmission, _____ , order selection, _____ , and customer delivery.

3. Often, this means that marketing and sales would like to maintain a broad product line with high inventory _____ each product's actual profit potential.

4. The _____ that physical distribution deals with customer requirements means that related operations will _____ than characteristic of manufacturing support and procurement performance cycles.

5. Physical distribution _____ should be designed to be as _____ as possible.

6. The producer also may _____ the number of retail outlets if the product requires specialized servicing or _____ .

II. Please complete the following table to get yourself familiar with the information on types of distribution.

Type of distribution	Appropriate customers	Appropriate products

III. Questions for discussion.

1. Please explain the physical distribution performance cycle.
2. Discuss and compare three approaches of distribution: intensive distribution, selective distribution, and exclusive distribution.
3. Why do we say that physical distribution links a firm with its customers?

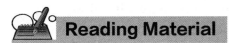

Logistics Distribution + Consumption Upgrading and Mode Innovation

In the past few years, e-commerce has undergone such drastic changes that shopping online has become popular among people from urban to rural. When shopping online developing as a routine consuming way in people's daily life, the categories of purchased products have been greatly extended from the garment, consumer electronics and computer to convenient goods, home appliance and decorative materials. The progressive improvement of channels online and the enormous abundance of product categories have greatly promoted the logistics market, in which the demands have been fragmented and diversified. It also calls for higher requirements on fineness and accuracy of delivery service. Nevertheless, the present service system is obviously becoming worse and worse to meet the ever-growing demands for logistics distribution.

(1) The tidal phenomenon in distribution orders.

The convenience and improvement of channels online together with the enormous abundance of product categories have made it possible for consumers to shop at anytime and anywhere, which have changed the original purchasing habits of shopping once a week or month so that elasticity of demand in society becomes bigger. These are the reasons for the tidal **phenomenon** in distribution orders, which means the present distribution resources have not been optimized and utilized efficiently.

(2) The rapidly increased costs in logistics distribution.

At initial stage of e-commerce in China, the purchased product categories are mainly made of 3C electronics or garment with higher unit price and smaller volume. While with the development of consumption upgrading, more and more orders online are becoming daily convenience products such as food, drinks with lower unit price but larger volume. For this, it is inevitable for logistics enterprises to face the problem of balancing the relationship between increasing logistics costs and customer service. With increasingly more scattered commercial outlets, worse traffic in cities, higher rent costs in warehousing and rapidly raising expenses on labor and gas, it is difficult to cover costs by profits. As a result, the whole logistics industry finds it hard to develop and provide quality service while it has to cut costs.

(3) The increased demands for experience consumption.

When the kids born in the 80s and 90s, who seek uniqueness, convenience and self-concern, have grown as the main consuming group, the ultimate purpose of their purchases is to build a better individual through enjoying service but not the product itself. Therefore, their living habits and consuming psychology guide their new consuming habit—pursuit of convenience and experience, which requires manufacturing industry to focus on not only optimization on product quality but also the **ecology** of the whole supply chain. Conforming to the trend of consumption upgrading, to build the products and service habits suitable to the preferences of main consuming group coordinately is an utmost important process in logistics distribution. It is discovered that college students born in 1994—1996 care more about some items such as service provided by logistics, coverage rate of outlets, convenience degree, service experience and delivery charges. There obviously exists a big difference between the requirement of consumers and service degree of logistics companies at present. Especially with the requirement of convenience and experience becoming higher and higher, the logistics industry has to adjust its operation mode **accordingly**. Besides, inefficient response, high logistics charges and unsatisfied experience from community customers are also the biggest troubles to logistics companies.

【Key Words】

upgrading [ˌʌˈgreidiŋ]	v.	升级；提高档次（upgrade 的现在分词）
innovation [ˌinəˈveiʃn]	n.	创新，革新；新方法
phenomenon [fəˈnɑːminən]	n.	现象；奇迹；杰出的人才
ecology [iˈkɑːlədʒi]	n.	生态学；社会生态学
accordingly [əˈkɔːdiŋli]	adv.	因此，于是；相应地

【Questions】

Describe one of your online shopping distribution claims and explain the reason.

Chapter 8
Green Logistics

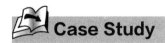 **Case Study**

【参考音频】

Good for the Environment, Good for Business

Today's leading companies, large and small, are looking for ways to go green. They understand that if we want our planet to remain **habitable** for generations to come, we must work together now to identify and reduce **emissions**, make our businesses more **sustainable** and ultimately move toward a Circular Economy.

Logistics plays a central role in the global economy and therefore the industry can play a crucial part in the way business is done with regard to the environmental impact. That's also one reason why we've made it our mission to achieve zero emissions by 2050 and be the industry benchmark for responsible business practices.

DHL is a pioneer of green logistics. We utilize our expertise to make your logistics greener and more sustainable—giving you an edge over the competition. We can also help you find ways to apply circular-economy principles to eradicate waste and retain more of the value that goes into your products.

1. Climate Neutral

DHL offered global Climate Neutral shipment services to a customer in the financial services sector—a business where vital overnight express shipments result in significant emissions. The goal was to make 95% of the bank's international courier services climate neutral, and the result was significant annual carbon savings, not to mention an enhanced brand image. What's more, the carbon credits purchased to offset emissions had no impact on the bank's operations, while the climate protection projects funded with those credits have had a huge impact on local populations.

2. Green Optimization—Warehousing

In the United States, a customer working across multiple sectors wanted to build a 250,000-square-foot sustainable distribution center with environmentally responsible design elements and efficient operating systems. The challenge was to design a facility with energy efficient lighting, sky lights, low-flow plumbing, a white roof system, storm water runoff containment, and a recycling program. Close coordination with local city authorities and the local development foundation added to the job's complexity. In the end, the new distribution center ensures a healthier environment for residents, workers and the local community through minimized energy and water consumption, reduced greenhouse gas emissions and reduced costs. Furthermore, the center achieved Leadership in Energy and Environmental Design (LEED) certification from the U.S. Green Building Council.

3. Green Optimization—Waste Recycling

A UK airline wanted to design an innovative in-flight catering and waste solution and asked DHL to help. We **benchmarked** waste rates and came up with a plan to minimize waste to landfill that included the installation of food dryers, a step that reduced the volume of food by 70%. Zero waste to landfill was achieved alongside a 70% reduction in food waste transport costs, significant added value from recovered waste, **substantial** recycling revenue, and eliminated landfill taxes.

Chapter 8 Green Logistics

【Key Words】

habitable [ˈhæbitəbl]	adj.	可居住的；适于居住的
emissions [iˈmiʃnz]	n.	排放；辐射；发行（emission 的复数形式）
sustainable [səˈsteinəbl]	adj.	可持续的；合理利用的
benchmark [ˈbentʃmɑrk]	n.	基准；标准检查程序
	vt.	用基准问题测试
substantial [səbˈstænʃl]	n.	本质；重要材料
	adj.	大量的；实质的

【Questions】

1. What is the definition of green logistics?
2. Can you illustrate other factors influencing green logistics by giving examples?

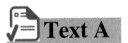 Text A

Green Logistics

Green logistics is an answer to one of the greatest struggles in the 21st century: the one between business and **sustainability**. In an environmentally conscious world, businesses are finding it beneficial to improve their environmental impact.[1] When they **undertake** that effort from manufacturing to distribution to consumption, they practice green logistics.

Green logistics focuses on materials handling, waste management, packaging and transport. Reverse logistics(see Text B) is a term sometimes used **interchangeably** with green logistics because it refers to the recycling and reuse of materials after they are successfully distributed to their destination.

The main objective of green logistics is to **coordinate** the activities within a supply chain in such a way that **beneficiary** needs are met at "least cost" to the environment.[2] It is a principle component of reverse logistics. In the past "cost" has been defined in **purely monetary** terms, whereas "cost" can now also be understood as the external costs of logistics associated with: climate change, air pollution, **dumping** waste (including packaging waste), soil **degradation**, noise, **vibration** and accidents.

Green or sustainable logistics is concerned with reducing environmental and other negative impacts associated with the movement of supplies. Sustainability seeks to ensure that decisions made today do not have an adverse impact on future generations. Green supply chains seek to reduce negative impact by redesigning **sourcing**, distribution systems and managing reverse logistics so as to eliminate any inefficiency, unnecessary freight movements and dumping of packaging.

A good example of one logistics aspect that poses great risk to the environment is packaging. Packaging represents one of the greatest challenges to environmental friendly logistics while at the same time being vital in shipping and storage.

Correct or incorrect packaging has consequences for how much of a product can be stored, how it is stored and or transported in a given space. This can increase to the unit cost if the packaging **hinders optimization** of storage space. Many industries have developed forms of packaging that do all that is required of them in transit but do not justify the expense of returning them to the point of origin. This packaging is only used once and then **discarded**. This principle goes all the way down to the level of individual tins or cartons of food.

It is this type of packaging that presents the greatest challenge to logistician as, increasingly, there is a responsibility for the supplier and the buyer to recover and recycle or effectively dispose of packaging.

Here are a few companies currently applying green logistics:

(1) Shiply—It is a British company founded on the idea that the current way goods are shipped to houses is wasteful. The company simply pairs returning trucks that would otherwise be empty with new orders.

(2) DHL—The well known shipping company offers a GOGREEN program that tracks the amount of CO_2 emitted when a company uses DHL to transport merchandise. That way, the company can make informed decisions on how to best reduce carbon emissions.

(3) FedEx—Since 2010, FedEx has been committed to a green logistics focus. The company is increasing its use of sustainable energy through an electric and **hybrid** truck fleet.

These companies are taking steps toward an environmentally friendly business that saves money and appeals to customers who want to support sustainability.[3] There are many easy steps taken to implement green logistics in the company:

(1) Reduce package size. Many companies are undertaking R&D to decrease the amount of material used in packaging.

(2) Change modes of transportation. Shipping freight by rail or water is often more environmentally friendly than trucking.

(3) Reduce transportation distance during distribution. As of 2010, heavy trucking accounted for 17 percent of all petroleum used in the United States. By cooperating with the North American Council for Freight Efficiency, you could reduce your freight shipping costs and distances.

(4) Teach drivers eco-friendly techniques such as reducing time on the road by maximizing right turns and minimizing left turns.

(5) Centralize warehousing and optimize efficiency. Larger warehouses are more energy efficient, but lower inventory levels use less energy (heating, refrigeration, lighting, etc.). Switching to LED lighting in warehouses will also greatly reduce electricity costs.

By taking steps like these to make your company a leader in green logistics, you not only save money and gain market advantage, but also you may anticipate future environmental regulations. More importantly, you help create a sustainable business that will **thrive** in our ever-changing world.

【Key Words】

sustainability [sə,steinə'biləti]	n.	持续性，能维持性，永续性
undertake [,ʌndə'teik]	vt.	承担；承诺
interchangeably [intə'tʃeindʒəbli]	adv.	可交换地，可交替地
coordinate [kəu'ɔːdineit]	v.	使协调，使调和；搭配；使动作协调
	adj.	同等的，并列的
beneficiary [,beni'fiʃəri]	n.	受益人
purely ['pjuəli]	adv.	完全地，十足地；纯粹地
monetary ['mʌnitri]	adj.	货币的，金钱的；金融的；财政的
dump [dʌmp]	vt.	倾倒；卸下；摆脱；转存；倾销
degradation [,degrə'deiʃn]	n.	堕落；降解；恶化
vibration [vai'breiʃn]	n.	摆动；震动；感受
sourcing ['sɔːsiŋ]	n.	采购

hinder ['hɪndə(r)]	v.	阻碍，妨碍；成为阻碍
optimization ['ɔptəmai'zeiʃən]	n.	最佳化，最优化；优选法；优化组合
discard [di'skɑːd]	vt.	丢弃，抛弃；解雇
hybrid ['haibrid]	n.	混合物，混合词
thrive [θraiv]	vi.	兴盛，兴隆；长得健壮

【Notes to Text A】

[1] In an environmentally conscious world, businesses are finding it beneficial to improve their environmental impact.

固定搭配：find it beneficial to do sth.

套用搭配：find it + adj. to do sth.

[2] The main objective of green logistics is to coordinate the activities within a supply chain in such a way that beneficiary needs are met at "least cost" to the environment.

句式：the objective is to do sth.

引申：the aim/purpose is to do sth.

[3] These companies are taking steps toward an environmentally friendly business that saves money and appeals to customers who want to support sustainability.

environmentally friendly 环保的，环境友好的

【Exercises to Text A】

I. Fill in the blanks.

1. Green supply chains seek to reduce negative impact by _____ sourcing, distribution systems and managing _____ logistics so as to eliminate any inefficiency, unnecessary freight movements and dumping of packaging.

2. Many industries have developed forms of packaging that do all that is required of them in but do not _____ the expense of returning them to the point of _____.

3. The main objective of green logistics is to _____ the activities within a supply chain in such a way that _____ needs are met at "least cost" to the environment.

4. These companies are taking steps toward a _____ business that saves money and appeals to customers who want to support _____.

5. Teach drivers _____ techniques such as reducing time on the road by maximizing right turns and minimizing left turns.

6. By taking steps like these to make your company a leader in green logistics, you not only save money and gain market advantage, but you may _____ future environmental regulations.

II. True or false.

1. Green logistics is the same meaning as reverse logistics. (　　)

2. FedEx offers a GOGREEN program that tracks the amount of CO_2 emitted when a company uses FedEx to transport merchandise. (　　)

3. Shipping freight by trucking is often more environmentally friendly than rail or water. (　　)
4. Larger warehouses are more energy efficient, but lower inventory levels use less energy. (　　)

III. Translation.

1. 绿色物流包括物流作业环节和物流管理全过程的绿色化。

2. 改进物流体系，既要考虑正向物流环节的绿色化，又要考虑供应链上的逆向物流体系的绿色化。

3. 绿色物流的最终目标是可持续性发展，实现该目标的准则是经济利益、社会利益和环境利益的统一。

4. 绿色物流是指以降低对环境的污染、减少资源消耗为目标，利用先进物流技术规划和实施的运输、储存、包装、装卸、流通加工等物流活动。

5. 要想打造绿色物流，首先要对运输线路进行合理布局与规划，通过缩短运输路线、提高车辆装载率等措施，实现节能减排的目标。

6. 绿色仓储一方面要求仓库选址要合理，有利于节约运输成本；另一方面，仓储布局要科学，使仓库得以充分利用，实现仓储面积利用的最大化，减少仓储成本。

7. 绿色物流建设应该起始于产品设计阶段，以产品生命周期分析等技术提高产品整个生命周期环境绩效，在推动绿色物流建设上发挥先锋作用。

8. 绿色包装要醒目环保，还应符合"4R"要求，即少耗材（Reduction）、可再用（Reuse）、可回收（Reclaim）和可再循环（Recycle）。

9. 绿色物流的关键所在，不仅依赖绿色物流观念的树立、绿色物流经营的推行，而且离不开绿色物流技术的应用和开发。

Reverse Logistics

Many organizations and individuals have tried to define **reverse logistics**. We refer to the term "reverse logistics" as all activity associated with a product/service after the point of sale, the ultimate goal to **optimize** or make more efficient aftermarket activity, thus saving money and environmental resources.

Reverse logistics **stands for** all operations related to the reuse of products and materials. It is "the process of planning, implementing, and controlling the efficient, cost effective flow of raw materials, in-process inventory, finished goods and related information from the point of consumption to the point of origin for the purpose of recapturing value or proper disposal. More precisely, reverse logistics is the process of moving goods from their typical final destination for the purpose of capturing value, or proper disposal. Remanufacturing and refurbishing activities also may be included in the definition of reverse logistics". The reverse logistics process includes the management and the sale of surplus as well as returned equipment and machines from the hardware leasing business. Normally, logistics deal with events that bring the product towards the customer. In the case of reverse logistics, the resource goes at least one step back in the supply chain.[1] For instance, goods move from the customer to the distributor or to the manufacturer.

Although reverse logistics has become a necessary business activity in almost all industries, most companies still concentrate their efforts on getting products out the door and to the customer.[2] The focal point of many contemporary supply chain logistics is sales and planning of the **outbound** process, from raw materials to manufacturing to final **consumption**. But firms are beginning to realize that reaching the final customer does not necessarily represent the end of the journey for a product.

Products flow backward after reaching their point of consumption for numerous reasons. A recent study reported that 51.65% of apparel companies agree to take back returned apparel

Chapter 8　Green Logistics

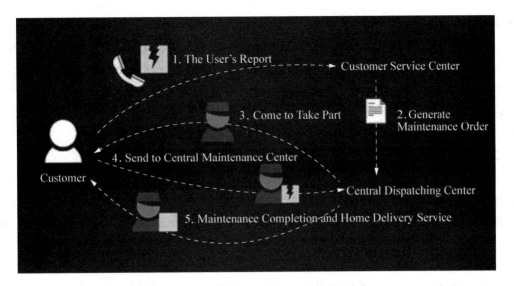

because it is **defective** or it was damaged in shipment. Approximately 48% take back merchandise, not because it was defective, but because the wrong model or size was purchased. Other apparel companies report that they take back product in an effort to maintain customer satisfaction and loyalty as well as to create good will.

After considerable **trials** and **tribulations**, companies have developed some simple and effective strategies for setting up a successful reverse logistics process.

1. Security

Returns should be separated from items bound for distribution. One of the main reasons is related to security. It is recommended that the reverse logistics area be designed to have only one entry and exit point.[3]

Return items sent back by mail are often lost or misplaced, resulting in poor customer service because of delays in charge backs, **erosion** of the company's reputation and financial loss. If the budget allows—metal **detectors** and personal security agents can also **drastically** minimize the number of lost or misplaced returns.

2. Shipping and Receiving

A common problem is the unloading of returns at the incorrect location within the distribution center. In this returned products can block the flow of outgoing merchandise. The returns can also be mixed with new products waiting to be shipped out. It takes time to sort through the merchandise mix. Returns often have to be **manually** returned to the correct area. To avoid this complication, a separate mailing address should be assigned to the returns dock.

3. Labor

Returns inspection is considered to be the most complicated function performed in reverse logistics. Numerous requirements regarding the condition of the returned product have to be **accounted for** by the inspectors. Better educated, better trained, and highly motivated employees are necessary to fill the positions.

The work load involved with returns is **unpredictable**. It has been found that establishing a mix of full-time and hourly workers for handling returns is a successful way to handle **labor utilization**. One company found success by hiring all returns inspectors as full-time employees, and hiring support personnel to unload returns, palletize and distribute the returns to the inspection stations, and pick and pack the processed returns according to **disposition** options. The support personnel are hourly wage employees. The rationale is that it is much easier to hire additional support employees than returns inspectors because they are not as highly trained.

4. The Return Policy

Companies should have a clear policy format regarding returns. The policy should include basic return guidelines for return authorization information, return product **eligibility** requirements, return shipping guidelines, freight damage guidelines, and a general corporate policy regarding returns. The return policy should be carefully communicated to customers.

5. Inspect Returns

Return inspectors should practice a systematic process. It is beneficial for each inspector to have their own personal code to ensure strict and personal **accountability**. Products should contain electrical profiles with pertinent information such as the manufacturer's number, the product's serial number, invoice number, etc. . Inspection involves comparing the data with the physical condition of the product.

6. Assign Disposition

The task of deciding what will be done with processed returns is known as assigning disposition. There are three major disposition categories—sell at a discount on **secondary** markets; return to the manufacturer/supplier; and return to stock/sellable.

Selling at a discount on secondary markets entails selling products that are in good operational condition, but which are packed in containers that have been damaged and /or compromised or have the manufacturer's seal broken.

It is helpful to use the term "secondary" to distinguish the difference between returned products and new products. The term "secondary" indicates that they have already been sold as new and are now going back to the market for the second time. For some companies, website selling has been a successful venue to resell secondary products.

Return to manufacturer/supplier entails pushing returned product back to manufacturers/suppliers—because of the implications of direct cost this is considered the highest priority concerning disposition options. Does the product have to be factory sealed? Return to stock/sellable is the final option. These returns are considered new with the original manufacturer's seal intact. A return stock/sellable product is placed back in inventory and sold as new. This is the preferred option for manufacturers and suppliers, since returns transportation costs are avoided and valuable inventory space is preserved.

The obvious reason for neglecting to implement a **state-of-the-art** reverse logistics program is cost related. Companies are already hard pressed to cut costs—including logistics **expenditures**—to a minimum; dealing with returns is considered an unnecessary and costly effort. However, the cost of not dealing with returns can be extremely costly.

Liberal customer service policies, along with rapid product **obsolescence** resulting from ever-shortening product life cycles, have made product returns a daily headache for many retailers. Before returns begin building up in the distribution center, slowing down the supply chain and negatively affecting the bottom line, it is **prudent** to implement clear and **cogent** strategies which will ease the return process as well as build customer satisfaction.

【Key Words】

reverse logistics		循环型物流
optimize ['ɔptimaiz]	vt.	使最优化，使尽可能有效
stand for		代表，表示；为……而奋斗；拥护
outbound ['autbaund]	adj.	开往外地的，开往外国的；向外的，出港的
consumption [kən'sʌmpʃn]	n.	消费，消耗量
defective [di'fektiv]	adj.	有缺陷的；不完美的，有缺点的
trial ['traiəl]	n.	审判，审理；测试，试验
tribulation [ˌtribju'leiʃn]	n.	苦难，艰难；苦难的缘由
erosion [i'rəuʒn]	n.	腐蚀，侵蚀，磨损；削弱，减少
detector [di'tektə]	n.	探测器，侦察器，检测器
drastically ['drɑːstikli]	adv.	彻底地；激烈地
manually ['mænjuəli]	adv.	用手地，手工地
account for		说明（解释）……原因；对……负有责任
unpredictable [ˌʌnpri'diktəbl]	adj.	无法预言的；捉摸不透的；不可预测的
labor utilization		劳动力使用

disposition [ˌdɪspəˈzɪʃn]	n.	性格；排列，布置；倾向	
eligibility [ˌelɪdʒəˈbləti]	n.	资格；合格	
accountability [əˌkaʊntəˈbɪləti]	n.	有责任，有义务	
secondary [ˈsekəndəri]	adj.	次要的，次等的；中级的；中学的	
state-of-the-art	adj.	最先进技术的，最高水平的	
expenditure [ɪkˈspendɪtʃə(r)]	n.	花费，使用；耗费，消耗	
liberal [ˈlɪbərəl]	n.	宽容的人，开明的人；自由主义者	
obsolescence [ˌɒbsəˈlesns]	n.	废弃，陈旧，过时	
prudent [ˈpruːdnt]	adj.	审慎的，精明的；判断力强的	
cogent [ˈkəʊdʒənt]	adj.	（理由、论据）有说服力的，令人信服的	

【Notes to Text B】

[1] In the case of reverse, the resource goes at least one step back in the supply chain.

in the case of 在……情况下

区别：in case 以防，万一

[2] Although reverse logistics has become a necessary business activity in almost all industries, most companies still concentrate their efforts on getting products out the door and to the customer.

although… still… 尽管……仍然……

[3] It is recommended that the reverse logistics area be designed to have only one entry and exit point.

句式"it is recommended that… (should) be"表示虚拟语态。

【Exercises to Text B】

I. Choose the best answer.

1. Reverse logistics stands for all operations related to the (　　) of products and materials.
   A. use B. reuse
   C. remove D. move

2. (　　) and refurbishing activities also may be included in the definition of reverse logistics.
   A. Manufacturing B. Remanufacturing
   C. Damaging D. Moving

3. In the case of reverse, the resource goes at least (　　) step back in the supply chain.
   A. one B. two
   C. three D. four

4. Products flow backward after reaching their point of (　　) for numerous reasons.
   A. distribution B. delivery
   C. warehousing D. consumption

5. After (　　) trials and tribulations, companies have developed some simple and effective strategies for setting up a successful reverse logistics process.
   A. considerate B. considerable
   C. less D. few

6. Returns should be (　　) items bound for distribution.

Chapter 8 Green Logistics

    A. added to   B. related to
    C. separated from   D. in addition to

7. The support (　　) are hourly wage employees.
    A. personnel   B. personal
    C. professional   D. human

8. It is (　　) for each inspector to have their own personal code to ensure strict and personal accountability.
    A. harmful   B. important
    C. interesting   D. beneficial

II. Reading and answering questions.

    Nowadays, most companies are familiar with the idea of "mission statement" as an expression of setting a vision for the business. The mission statement seeks to define the purpose of the business, its boundaries and its aspirations. It is now common for organizations to have such statement for the business as a whole and for key constituent components. What some companies have found is that there can be significant benefits to defining the logistics vision of the firm.

    The purpose of the logistics vision statement is to give a clear indication which business intends to build a position of advantage through closer customer relationship. Such statement is never easy to construct. There is always the danger that they will publish the energetic and encouraging declaration that give everyone a warm feeling but provide no guideline for action.

    Ideally the logistics vision should be built around the simple issue of "how do we intend to use logistics and supply chain management to create value for our customers?" To realize this idea will necessitate a detailed understanding of how customer value is created and delivered in the market in which the business competes. Value chain analysis will be a fundamental element in this investigation as will the definition of the core competencies and capabilities of the organization. Asking the question "what activities do we excel in?" and "what is it that differentiates us from our competitors?" is the starting point for creating the logistics vision statement?

    Earlier, it was suggested that the three words "Better, Faster, Cheaper" summarizes the ways in which logistics vision statement can provide value for customers. The criterion for good logistics vision statement is that it should provide the road map for how these three goals are to be achieved.

    Questions:

1. What does mission statement intend to do? (　　)
    A. To please management.
    B. To define, summarize and achieve a common goal.
    C. To achieve higher market share and profitability.
    D. To develop new markets.

2. What kind of goals may the mission statement fail to achieve? (　　)
    A. To provide realistic guidelines to guide the actions to achieve results.
    B. To design a goal that everyone agrees.
    C. To point out a good goal.
    D. To implement effectively.

3. Which element should a logistics mission statement focus on? (　　)
    A. Transportation.   B. Costs.

C. Customers.   D. Punctuality.
4. How should a logistics vision statement add value to its customers? ( )
   A. To provide cheaper services.
   B. To provide more choices for transportation.
   C. To communicate better with customers.
   D. To provide better, more cost-effective and punctual services.
5. What should a logistics mission statement provide? ( )
   A. Management encouragement.
   B. A design of new methods to apply to customer satisfaction.
   C. Some detailed actions to undertake to obtain more market share.
   D. An outline of actions for goals to be achieved.

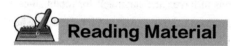

A Blueprint for Green Logistics

Although the environment is not a major **preoccupation** or priority in the industry itself, reverse distribution has opened up new market possibilities based upon growing societal concerns over waste disposal and recycling. Here the environmental benefits are derived rather than direct. The transportation industry itself does not present a greener face, indeed in a literal sense reverse logistics adds further to the traffic load. The manufacturers and domestic waste producers are the ones achieving the environmental credit. Pressures are mounting from a number of directions that are moving all actors and sectors in the economy in the direction of increasing regard for the environment. In some sectors this is already manifest, in others, such as the logistics industry, it is latent. The issue is when and in what form it will be realized. Three scenarios are possible. While not mutually exclusive, they each present different approaches and implications:

(1) A top-down approach where "greenness" is imposed on the logistic industry by government policies.

(2) A bottom-up approach where environmental improvements are coming from the industry itself.

(3) A compromise between the government and industry, notably through certification.

First is that government action will force a green agenda on the industry, in a top-down approach. Although this the least desirable outcome for the logistics industry, it is already evident that government intervention and **legislation** are reaching ever more directly over environmental issues. In Europe, there is a growing interest in charging for external costs, as the EU moves towards a "fair and efficient" pricing policy. A sharp increase in costs could have a more serious impact than a more gradual, phased-in tax. In North America, there is a growing interest in road pricing, with the re-appearance of tolls on new highways and bridges built by the private sector, and by congestion pricing, especially in metropolitan areas.

Pricing is only one aspect of government intervention. Legislation controlling the movement of hazardous goods, reducing packaging waste, stipulating the recycled content of products, the **mandatory** collection and recycling of products are already evident in most jurisdictions. Indeed, it is such legislation that has given rise to the reverse logistics industry. Truck safety, driver education, limits on driver's time at the wheel, are among many types of government action with a potential to impact the logistics industry.

A difficulty with government intervention is that the outcomes are often unpredictable, and in an industry as complex as logistics, many could be unexpected and unwanted. Environmentally-inspired policies may impact on freight and passenger traffic differentially, just as different modes may experience widely variable results of a common regulation. Issues concerning the greenness of logistics extend beyond transport regulations. The sitting of terminals and warehouses are crucial to moving the industry towards the goal of sustainability, yet these are often under the land use and zoning control of lower levels of government whose environmental interests may be at variance with national and international bodies.

If a top-down approach appears inevitable, in some respects at least, a bottom-up solution would be the industry preference. Its leaders oppose leaving the future direction to be shaped by government action. There are several ways a bottom-up approach might come about. As with reverse logistics, these occur when the business interests of the industry match the imperatives of the environment. One such match is the concern of the logistics industry with empty moves. With the growing sophistication of fleet management and IT control over scheduling and routing, further gains are achievable.

Less predictable, but with a much greater potential impact on the greenness of the industry, are possible attitudinal changes within logistics and without. These changes are comparable of that which has already occurred in recycling. There has emerged striking public support for domestic recycling. This has been extended by some firms in successfully marketing their **compliance** and adoption of green strategies. Firms have found that by advertising their friendliness towards the environment and their compliance with environmental standards, they can obtain an edge in the marketplace over their competitors. Traditionally, price and quality characteristics formed the basis of choice, but because environment preservation is seen as desirable in general, greenness can become a competitive advantage. Ultimately, pressure from within the industry can lead to greater environmental awareness and respect. Companies that stand apart will lose out because purchasers will demand environmental compliance.

Somewhere between the bottom-up and top-down approaches are the moves being implemented with environmental management systems. Although governments are involved in varying degrees, a number of voluntary systems are in place, notably ISO 14000 and EMAS (Environmental Management and Audit System). In these systems firms receive certification on the basis of establishing an environmental quality control tailored to that firm, and the setting up of environmental monitoring and accounting procedures. Obtaining certification is seen as evidence of the firm's commitment to the environment, and is frequently used as a public relations, marketing, and government relations advantage. This represents a fundamental commitment of the corporation to engage in environmental assessment and audit that represent a significant modification of traditional practices, in which efficiency, quality and cost evaluations prevailed.

It can be argued that the **paradoxes** of green logistics make it impossible for the logistics industry to become significantly greener. The internal inconsistencies between the goal of environmental sustainability and an industry that gives undue preference to road and air transport can be seen as being irreconcilable. Yet internal and external pressures promoting a more environmentally-friendly logistics industry appear to be inexorable. Of the three possible directions by which a greener logistics industry may emerge, it is realistic to consider that they will concomitantly help shape the industry of the future.

【Key Words】

preoccupation [priˌɔkjuˈpeiʃn]	n.	当务之急；抢先占据；成见
legislation [ˌledʒisˈleiʃn]	n.	立法；法律
mandatory [ˈmændətɔːri]	n.	受托
	adj.	强制的；托管的；命令的
compliance [kəmˈplaiəns]	n.	顺从，服从；符合；屈从；可塑性
paradoxes [ˈpærəˌdɔksiz]	n.	悖论（paradox 的复数形式）

【Questions】

1. How many approaches are mentioned in the passage? What are they?
2. In your opinion, which approach is the best?

Chapter 9
Integrated Logistics

【参考音频】

Supply Chain Integration Becomes a Reality

Customer-focused supply chains that can better **align** and link the various firms making up the supply chain are increasingly likely to gain **competitive advantage**. This can be **exemplified** by Walmart, Dell, and IBM examples. Supply chain **integration** with agreement on goals, business strategies, and **information transparency** can have **significant impacts** on capacity investment, inventories, design, responsiveness, and support of a firm's worldwide product/service development, operations/manufacturing, and sourcing footprints.

An example, discussed here in more detail, is the Motorola supply chain integration. In 2005, Motorola undertook the task of linking the various elements that make up its supply chains worldwide. The objectives were cost, cash, and customer service. Cost competitiveness would enable competitive pricing, cash would enable business investment, and customer service would enable the **retention** of customers.

The challenge was significant, as Motorola operates worldwide. Sales **spanned** all regions of the globe and purchases came from suppliers in 47 countries (as of 2004), and in the past the six business units generally did little sharing of resources or **facilities**.

To achieve transformation to an integrated supply chain, the focus was to align and link product design, **procurement**, manufacturing, logistics, and customer service. In addition, the following six key steps provide a high-level process approach to implement the change:

(1) Identify best-in-class processes for **duplication** throughout the company.

(2) Develop a supply base that has been right-sized and improve working relationships with key suppliers.

(3) Establish **clear-cut** supplier quality expectations and provide performance feedback via a **performance scorecard**.

(4) Establish most effective and efficient manufacturing and logistics operations.

(5) Focus information technology improvement projects to maximize the impact across all business units.

(6) Create an **action-oriented** and **results-driven** culture.

The results of the transformation by 2007 were dramatic. Examples are the following:

(1) Various teams identified best-in-class practices and the highest-priority practices were implemented worldwide.

(2) Business units work collaboratively to solicit quotes and award business.

(3) Suppliers were required to develop "quality renewal plans" to continue to do work with Motorola, and Motorola provided performance data to suppliers.

(4) Motorola's manufacturing and distribution operations square footage was reduced by 40% by examining its worldwide footprint and consolidating facilities.

(5) 90% of Motorola's information technology spend is now on systems that are common and help all business units—not just one.

(6) In addition, a number of achievements as of year-end 2006 include reduced ppm defects from suppliers by 50%; achieved customer on-time deliveries of 85% to 92% at some business

units (up from 30% to 40%); improved material expenses, product quality, and manufacturing efficiency by 40%; and achieved an 18% improvement in inventory turns.

【Outline】

Overall, this example suggests that a focused effort on integrating the vertical or functional silos into a more integrated supply chain(s) can produce performance results. This supply chain integration is a major ongoing challenge and will be the focus of future efforts.

【Key Words】

align [əˈlaɪn]	v.	与……联合，结盟；对准，校直
competitive advantage		竞争优势，比较优势
exemplify [ɪɡˈzemplɪfaɪ]	v.	例证，例示；典范
integration [ˌɪntɪˈɡreɪʃn]	n.	集成；综合，整合；一体化
information transparency		信息透明
significant impact		重大影响
retention [rɪˈtenʃn]	n.	保留，扣留，滞留；记忆力
span [spæn]	n.	跨度，跨距；范围；持续时间
	vt.	跨越；持续；包括，涵盖
facilities [fəˈsɪlɪtiz]	n.	设施；工具，设备（facility 的复数形式）
procurement [prəˈkjʊəmənt]	n.	采购；获得，取得
duplication [ˌdjuːplɪˈkeɪʃn]	n.	复制；重复
clear-cut	adj.	清晰的；明确的
performance scorecard		绩效记分卡
action-oriented	adj.	以行动为导向的
result-driven	adj.	以结果为驱动的，以结果为导向的

 Text A

Integrated Logistics

Integrated logistics is **defined** as the process of **anticipating** customer needs and wants; **acquiring** the **capital**, materials, people, technologies, and information necessary to meet those needs and wants; **optimizing** the goods or service—producing a network to **fulfill** customer requests; and utilizing the network to fulfill customer requests in a timely way.[1]

Integration has been one of the development of logistics management. This development began around 40 years ago at a **local** level. Today, many businesses are making **efforts** to integrate global supply networks, comprise several tiers of supplier and distributor, and use different transport modes and carries.[2]

Basically, the integrated international logistics management concept refers to administering the various activities as an integrated system. In firms that have not adopted a systems approach, logistics is often a **fragmented** and **uncoordinated** set of activities spread throughout various organizational functions, with each individual function having its own budget, set of priorities, and measurement system.[3]

A number of firms, such as Herman Miller, 3M, and Whirlpool Corporation, have found that total logistics costs can be reduced by integrating such logistic-related activities as customer service, transportation, warehousing, inventory management, order processing and information systems, and production planning and purchasing.

The performance of international logistics could be complex and **roundabout**. For example, one firm buys the raw silk in China, weaves it in Republic of Korea, prints it in Italy and sells it in the United States market.

The payment from the buyer to the seller causes the flow of paperwork with the goods flowing. The international logistics means a system in which documentation flows are as much a part of the main logistical flow as flows of goods. The transaction channel handles contracting and trading, whereas the logistics channel deals with the physical movement of goods. The channels are separated from each other, that is, a firm may locate sales offices in a different set of cities than where it locates distribution center. However, the two channels are linked to the extent that sales, or payments, release of goods to the buyer.

Chapter 9　Integrated Logistics

　　The integration of international logistics can improve the international flow of inventory, international transport and warehouse asset utilization, and often eliminates the **duplication of effort**.[4] For example, rather than having the purchasing department negotiate with inbound carriers and the logistics department negotiate with outbound carriers, one organization can negotiate for both inbound and outbound transportation. The central **coordination** of the various logistics activities forces cost **trade-offs** to be made between and among logistics activities such as customer service, transportation, warehousing, inventory management, order processing, product planning, and purchasing.

【Key Words】

integrated ['intigreitid]	adj.	综合的；完整的，整体的
define [di'fain]	v.	阐明；限定；给……下定义
anticipate [æn'tisipeit]	vt.	预期，预计；期望，期盼
acquire [ə'kwaiə(r)]	vt.	获得，购得
capital ['kæpitəl]	n.	首都，首府；中心
	adj.	首都的；重要的
optimize ['ɔptimaiz]	vt.	使最优化，使尽可能有效
fulfill [ful'fil]	vt.	履行，实现，完成（计划等）
local ['ləukl]	adj.	地方的，当地的；局部的
	n.	本地人；局部
effort ['efət]	n.	努力，成就
fragmented [fræg'mentid]	adj.	成碎片的，片段的
uncoordinated ['ʌnkəu'ɔːdineitid]	adj.	不协调的
roundabout ['raundəbaut]	adj.	迂回的；绕道的
duplication [,djuːpli'keiʃn]	n.	复制，重复
coordination [kəu,ɔːdineiʃn]	n.	协调，和谐；配合
trade-off	n.	交易；折中

【Notes to Text A】

　　[1] Integrated logistics is defined as the process of anticipating customer needs and wants; acquiring the capital, materials, people, technologies, and information necessary to meet those needs and wants; optimizing the goods or service—producing a network to fulfill customer requests; and utilizing the network to fulfill customer requests in a timely way.

　　对某事物下定义时，一般用被动语态，如"sth. is defined as…"。在本句中出现了 5 个动名词结构短语，这是因为这些动词都落在介词"of"的后面，变成名词短语而非独立句子。

[2] This development began around 40 years ago at a local level. Today, many businesses are making efforts to integrate global supply networks, comprise several tiers of supplier and distributor, and use different transport modes and carries.

"to integrate…, comprise…, and use…" 是不定式的一种，"to" 后面接多个并列的动词原形。

[3] In firms that have not adopted a systems approach, logistics is often a fragmented and uncoordinated set of activities spread throughout various organizational functions, with each individual function having its own budget, set of priorities, and measurement system.

"with each individual function having its own budget, set of priorities, and measurement system" 起 "with" 结构的副词作用，形式是 "with+ 宾语 + 现在分词或短语"。

[4] The integration of international logistics can improve the international flow of inventory, international transport and warehouse asset utilization, and often eliminates the duplication of effort.

介词短语 "of" 后面可接多个并列的名词，如 "inventory" "international transport" 和 "warehouse asset utilization" 等。

【Exercises to Text A】

I. Fill in the blanks.

1. The movement of _____ and _____ to a manufacturing company must be managed.
2. Integrated logistics is a _____ process.
3. The performance of international logistics could be _____.
4. However, the two channels are linked to the extent that sales, or _____ of goods to the buyer.
5. The integration of international logistics can improve the international flow of _____, international transport and warehouse asset utilization, and often eliminates the _____ of effort.

II. True or false.

1. Production lines sit idle if integrated logistics succeeds in transporting parts and raw materials into the plant. ( )
2. Operations need not produce goods if they can move efficiently and effectively to the market. ( )
3. Integrated logistics is more important than marketing or production. ( )
4. Integrated logistics requires goods to move, and it is useful to move goods that can be used or sold. ( )
5. Storing and protecting stopped goods incur cost with adding value. ( )

III. Translation.

1. 在交易双方处理合同和贸易的同时，物流部门处理货物的流转。

2. 一体化已成为物流管理发展的重要主题。

3. 国际物流的发展需要对各自分散的功能要素进行整合。

4. 国际物流中的整合能够提高存货的国际流转、国际运输和仓储资产利用程度。

5. 良好的国际物流系统能使跨国公司获得巨大的经济利益。

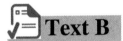 Text B

The Integrated Model of FedEx Corporation

FedEx Corporation is a US $20 billion market leader in transportation, information, and logistics solutions, providing strategic direction to six main operating companies.[1] These are FedEx Express, FedEx Ground, FedEx Freight, FedEx Custom Critical, FedEx Trade Networks, and FedEx Services.

Prior to the purchase of the ground, freight, and other **non-express-based** services, Federal Express had reorganized all of its major **indirect spend** in information technology, aircraft, facilities/business services, vehicles/fuel/ground service equipment, and supply chain logistics groups under the Strategic Sourcing and Supply group, led by Edith Kelly Green.

After the purchase of these different businesses, the supply management function was reorganized into a **center-led** supply chain management (SCM) sourcing model[2] ("center" refers to a Center of Excellence that focuses on centralizing sourcing strategy teams).

Over the last two years, FedEx Supply Chain Management has been focusing on leveraging sourcing and contracting for all of the FedEx family of companies.[3] For office supplies, instead of having each company run a contract, SCM has a single corporate contract for all of the **negotiation** effort that allows for different **transactional** approaches.

It has been a gradual **migration** to a centralized view of how **procurement** happens. It is central for the larger spend areas and different policy requirements. FedEx established a seven-step sourcing process as followings:

Step 1: A user provides a requisition for an item. When the user provides the requisition, the sourcing **specialist** or team must establish whether it is worth putting a strategy around it. This is typically done using a **return-on-investment criterion**: is the spend large enough to put a **significant** amount of time into sourcing the product through a **full-blown** supplier evaluation?[4] For example, if the requisition is for something that turns out to be a US $200,000 per year spend, the payback on it may not be worth the resources required to do a full supplier **evaluation** and selection process. However, if the spend is large enough, the team will conduct an assessment of the category that **profiles** that industry and commodity. This **assessment** involves researching the nature of existing purchasing activity: how much is it, who is it with, and what are the issues with existing suppliers? If it is not large enough, the user may be directed to a simple purchase order and invoice through the Ariba system.

Step 2: Assuming a large spend, based on research conducted in Step 1, the team goes into a process to select the sourcing strategy, **in essence** taking all of the information it has and deciding how it will approach that marketplace. Is a request for proposal appropriate? Does it need to maintain existing relationships or revisit negotiation and develop a strategy regarding the sourcing strategy?

Step 3: Assuming it is going beyond a negotiation, the team must conduct in-depth research with suppliers in that area, including qualification of the suppliers. Can the suppliers satisfy user requirements, service aspects, and so on? The end goal is to develop a list of suppliers to send RFPs①. The team conducts a supplier portfolio analysis.

Step 4: Another phase of this implementation pass is to revisit this strategy and have the team take another look at it. Has it uncovered something that will cause it to change negotiation? The team develops a strategy for negotiation, does it want to use a reverse auction or use a conventional RFP, as well as criteria for supplier evaluation? Is this still something it wants to do? If so, it proceeds with the RFP to the selected suppliers.

Step 5: After receiving RFPs, the team conducts the supplier selection and negotiation process.

Step 6: Once the team has made the selection, it needs to do the integration. This is done by applying the Ariba toolset with the supplier and identifying integration **conflicts** to be resolved to make the contract workable.

Step 7: The final stage in this process is to benchmark the supply market by monitoring the supplier(s) through the FedEx Supplier **Scorecard** system.

---

① RFPs　RFP 是 Request for Proposal 的缩写，即建议请求、意见书。RFPs 是 RFP 的复数形式。

Chapter 9 Integrated Logistics

【Key Words】

prior to		在……之前
non-express-based	adj.	非快递基础之上的
indirect spend		间接费用
center-led	n.	中央集权
negotiation [ˌniɡəʊʃiˈeiʃn]	n.	协商，谈判；转让；通过
transactional [trænˈzækʃənəl]	adj.	交易型的；事务性的
migration [maiˈɡreiʃn]	n.	迁移，移居；移动
procurement [prəˈkjuəmənt]	n.	采购；获得，取得
specialist [ˈspeʃəlist]	n.	专家；专科医生
return-on-investment	n.	投资收益
criterion [kraiˈtiəriən]	n.	（判定的）标准；准则，规范
significant [siɡˈnifikənt]	adj.	重要的；有效的；显著的
full-blown [fulˈbləun]	adj.	成熟的；（花）盛开的；充分发展的
evaluation [iˌvæljuˈeiʃn]	n.	评价，评估
profiles [ˈprəufailz]	n.	配置文件；剖面图；侧面（profile 的多数形式）
	v.	扼要描述；描绘轮廓
assessment [əˈsesmənt]	n.	评定；估价；看法
in essence		本质上
conflict [ˈkɒnflikts]	n.	争执，冲突；矛盾，分歧
	v.	抵触；冲突
scorecard [ˈskɔːkɑːd]	n.	记分卡

【Notes to Text B】

[1] FedEx Corporation is a US $20 billion market leader in transportation, information, and logistics solutions, providing strategic direction to six main operating companies.

"providing strategic direction to six main operating companies" 是现在分词短语作定语，修饰前面的表语 "market leader"。

[2] After the purchase of these different businesses, the supply management function was reorganized into a center-led supply chain management (SCM) sourcing model.

"was reorganized into" 是动词的过去分词表示被动形式。

[3] Over the last two years, FedEx Supply Chain Management has been focusing on leveraging sourcing and contracting for all of the FedEx family of companies.

"leveraging sourcing and contracting for…" 是动名词短语作宾语。

[4] This is typically done using a return-on-investment criterion: is the spend large enough to put a significant amount of time into sourcing the product through a full-blown supplier evaluation?

"return-on-investment" "full-blown" 都是复合词。

【Exercises to Text B】

I. Fill in the blanks.

1. FedEx Corporation is a US $20 billion _____ in transportation, information, and logistics solutions, providing strategic direction to six main operating companies.

2. _____ the purchase of the ground, freight, and other _____ services, Federal Express had reorganized all of its major _____ in information technology, aircraft, facilities/business services, vehicles/fuel/ground service equipment, and supply chain logistics groups under the Strategic Sourcing and Supply group, led by Edith Kelly Green.

3. After the purchase of these different businesses, the supply management function was reorganized into a _____ supply chain management (SCM) sourcing model.

II. Translation.

1. 在采购了这些不同的业务之后，供应管理的功能被重新整合成一个中央控制的供应链管理采购模式。

2. 最近两年以来，联邦快递供应链管理一直致力于平衡所有联邦快递子公司的采购和签约。

3. 假设将要有一场谈判，团队将对区域供应商及供应商资质进行深度调研。

4. 当使用方提出要求，公司资源专家或团队必须判定是否值得使用策略。

5. 投资回报可能无须启用完整供应商评估程序。

6. 从整个采购发生来看，这是一个走向集中管理的渐变过程。

III. Reading and answering questions.

Third party logistics providers are to lower the total cost of logistics for the supplier and improve the service level to the customer. Third party logistics have been growing rapidly. Cost reduction and demands

Chapter 9 Integrated Logistics

for better and cheaper services are the main drives behind the growth. A third party logistics provider will be in a position to consolidate business from several companies and offer frequent pick-ups and deliveries, whereas in-house transportation cannot. Other reasons are as follows:

(1) The company does not specialize in logistics.

(2) The company does not have sufficient resources.

(3) Eager to implement better logistics operation or does not have time to develop the required capabilities in-house.

(4) The company is venturing into a new business with totally different logistics requirements.

(5) Merger or acquisition may make outsourcing logistics operations more attractive than to integrate logistics operations.

Questions:

1. Third Party logistics provides (　　) logistics services.
   A. single   B. some
   C. simple   D. all of the above

2. Third party logistics is the (　　) between the supplier and customer.
   A. link   B. bridge
   C. middle   D. transport

3. The advantage of third party logistics are (　　).
   A. better service   B. lower cost
   C. overall   D. A and B

4. Third party logistics is more (　　) than other logistics provides in operations.
   A. quick   B. fast
   C. specialized   D. exact

5. What promotes the third party logistics developing its business? (　　)
   A. outsourcing   B. transporting
   C. warehousing   D. distribution

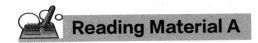

Reading Material A

Integration Meets Resistance

While the idea of functional integration is logical and **appeals to common sense**, it is not always supported by other unit managers. It is natural that any attempt to reposition management authority and responsibility will meet **resistance**. Many logistics executives can provide examples of how attempts to reorganize were met with **rivalry** and **mistrust**—not to mention **accusations** of empire building. Traditionally, in organizational structures, financial **budgets** follow operational responsibility. **Likewise**, power, visibility, and compensation result from managing large **head counts** and substantial budgets. Logistical reorganizations, therefore, was typically seen as a way for logistical managers to gain power, visibility, and compensation at the

133

expense of other managers. This also was an **ample** reason for other managers to protect their power by resisting logistics functional integration. As a result, unified logistical organizations faced considerable resistance. But in an increasing number of firms, benefits were sufficient to **empower** reorganization.

【Key Words】

appeal to		呼吁；对……有吸引力
common sense		常识
resistance [ri'zist(ə)ns]	n.	阻力；电阻；抵抗
rivalry ['raivlri]	n.	对抗；竞争，竞争行为
mistrust [ˌmis'trʌst]	n.	不信任；怀疑
	vt.	不信任；怀疑
accusation [ˌækjʊ'zeiʃn]	n.	控告，指控；谴责
budget ['bʌdʒit]	n.	预算，预算费
	adj.	廉价的
likewise ['laikwaiz]	adv.	同样地；也，而且
head count		人口调查
ample ['æmpl]	adj.	丰富的；足够的；丰满的
empower [im'paʊə(r)]	vt.	授权，允许；使能够

【Questions】

1. Why is functional integration not supported by other unit managers?
2. Give some examples of resistance to a firm's logistics functional integration.

Reading Material B

Major Food Safety Risks in China's Supply Chain

1. "Broken Cold Chain"

Cold chain logistics refers to systems which ensure that **refrigerated** & frozen foods are always in a standard, low temperature environment across the supply chain, from production to storage, to transportation and point of sale. In doing so, cold chain logistics help to ensure food quality and reduce food **spoilage**. Most foods, especially agricultural products and fresh food, are

perishable and require cold chain storage and transportation throughout the supply chain. Due to the length of the supply chain, with multiple transfer points and different storage and transportation environments, the cold chain system faces many uncontrollable factors that may result in a "Broken Cold Chain", either caused **intentionally** or **accidentally**. It could be very difficult to identify breaks along the supply chain. In Shanghai, a food safety incident occurred because of a disconnect along the cold chain, with the cause of the incident later being isolated to an accident involving a refrigerated vehicle.

2. Illegal Additives

Transportation over long distances can cause food spoilage. Live livestock, poultry, and aquatic products are especially vulnerable to long distances, as high packing densities and time may cause death. To reduce losses, some producers add drugs to animal feed, though these additives are against the law. As stipulated in the Food Safety Law, the use of preservatives in the packaging, preservation, storage or transportation of edible agricultural products must comply with national food safety standards.

3. Missing Information

According to the Food Safety Law, a national food safety whole supply-chain **traceability** system should be established. Food producers and operators are expected to establish a food safety tracking system to guarantee the traceability of food. Tracing food safety information from farm to table is dependent on transferring information across the supply chain, which is essential to ensure that the food source and destination can be traced and relevant stakeholders can be held accountable. If any part of the supply chain is "interrupted", or if any information is inaccurately transferred, information downstream may go missing.

4. Spreading Unlicensed Food

The Food Safety Law stipulates the implementation of a licensing system for the production and management of food. Permission is required to engage in food production, the sale of food, as well as catering services. The State Administration of Market Regulation (SAMR) formulated the Measures for the Administration of Food Production Licenses and Measures for the Administration of Food Business Licenses, which state the basic requirements for license applicants. Although the sale of agricultural products does not require an administrative license, the Opinions on Strengthening the Quality and Safety Supervision and Management of Edible Agricultural Products jointly issued by the Ministry of Agriculture and Rural Affairs and the China Food and Drug Administration clearly states management requirements for the production and sale of products to prevent unlicensed foods from entering the Chinese market. While a strong supply chain can promote fair trade in food, a poor supply chain may help facilitate the spread of potentially unsafe food, potentially bringing unlicensed food to market.

【Key Words】

refrigerated [riˈfridʒəreitid]	adj.	冷冻的，冷却的
	v.	冷藏（refrigerate 的过去分词）；使冷却
spoilage [ˈspɔilidʒ]	n.	损坏，糟蹋；掠夺；损坏物
perishable [ˈperiʃəbl]	n.	容易腐坏的东西
	adj.	易腐烂的；易变质的
intentionally [inˈtenʃənəli]	adv.	故意地；有意地
accidentally [ˌæksiˈdentəli]	adv.	意外地；偶然地
traceability [ˌtreisəˈbiləti]	n.	可追溯性；跟踪能力；可描绘

【Questions】

What strategies can be adopted to improve the quality in cold chain management?

Chapter 10
Logistics Documents

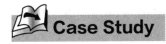

FedEx Trade Networks for Cargo Insurance

For more than a century, companies across North America have trusted FedEx Trade Networks for reliable customs **brokerage**, international freight forwarding and transportation.

Are your shipments fully protected in case of **disaster**? Do you really have enough coverage to protect the cargo that you are moving halfway around the world? Do you know when you are covered and when you are not covered? Don't find out the hard way that you don't have enough insurance. FedEx Trade Networks Transport & Brokerage, Inc. can **assist** you with cargo insurance that offers the best protection available at rates you can afford.

Many shippers misunderstand cargo insurance in particular and the insurance industry in general. Brokers assume that, because they purchased a "**contingency** cargo liability" policy, they will be **compensated** for all loss-and-damage claims. In fact, "**exclusions**", which can be found in the "endorsements" section of insurance policies, modify those policies to exclude the most frequent causes of transit claims. They also may exclude whatever recent **catastrophe** has led to a large number of claims payments.

Some policies cover only the period that the goods are in the **custody** of a "common carrier". Therefore, shippers must be certain that every form of transportation they use is covered, including contract carriage and private carriage, and that the policy covers the entire period from the time a shipment leaves the shipping dock until it is delivered to a customer.

Making sure that carriers have the right insurance policies presents a challenge because their policies are not very **accessible** to shippers. Carriers generally offer "Certificates of Insurance" to shippers as proof of coverage. However, these certificates contain a disclaimer of liability that applies if the issuer fails to notify the certificate holder of the **cancellation** or **modification** of the insurance coverage. More importantly, these certificates do not reveal the exclusions in the underlying policy. In addition to these common exclusions, motor carrier cargo policies contain a standard exclusion for "employee **infidelity**". For that reason, shippers should insist that all parties with whom they do business obtain a separate **fidelity** bond. Under the I.C.C.[①] Termination

---

① I.C.C. 伦敦保险协会货物保险条款（Institute Cargo Clause）的简称。目前，世界上大多数国家在海上保险业务中直接采用 I.C.C. 所制定的协会货物条款。

Chapter 10 Logistics Documents

Act, shippers are responsible for obtaining a copy of carriers' tariffs to determine the extent of their liability.

【Key Words】

brokerage ['brəukəridʒ]	n.	经纪人（中间人）业务；佣金；手续费
disaster [di'zɑ:stər]	n.	灾难；不幸
assist [ə'sist]	v.	帮助；援助；促进
contingency [kən'tindʒənsi]	n.	偶发事件；偶然；依附条件，制约条件
compensated ['kɔmpenseitid]	v.	补偿，报酬（compensate 的过去分词）；给（某人赔偿（赔款）
exclusion [ik'sklu:ʒn]	n.	排除；除外；排斥
catastrophe [kə'tæstrəfi]	n.	灾难；困难
custody ['kʌstədi]	n.	拘留；监禁；监护；羁押
accessible [ək'sesəbl]	adj.	可得到的；易接近的；可进入的；易理解的
cancellation [ˌkænsə'leiʃn]	n.	取消；撤销；作废
modification [ˌmɔdifi'keiʃn]	n.	修改；修正；修饰
infidelity [infi'deləti]	n.	无信仰；不忠实
fidelity [fi'deləti]	n.	忠实，忠诚；尽责；保真度

Text A

Electronic Delivery of Documents

In the modern world, the document software can be used to create, view, e-mail, and print the **formatted** document. Lots of logistics documents can be printed. <u>For example, an easy-to-use online bill of lading **generator** will save time and provide the documents **instantly**</u>.[1]

The electronic delivery of the bill of lading can speed up the trade financing process. <u>It can reduce the cycle time for forwarding and presentation of documents. The exporter gets paid more quickly and the importer gets title to the goods sooner.</u>[2] It also **eliminates** the risk of errors and reduces the costs related to manual document preparation.

A large number of documents are needed in the global transport. Logistics documents are **indispensable** in the logistics services, which mainly include letter of credit, bill of lading, **multimodal** transport documents, invoice, insurance policy, inspection certificate, certificate of origin, packing list, air waybill, shipper's export declaration, etc..

Documentation is an important area of logistics management. The major **characteristics** about documents are accurate, **integrated**, concise and timely. Accuracy means that the details of logistics documents must be fully **consistent** with that of sales contract, **ambiguous** words and expressions can't be used;[3] **integrity** is that all logistics documents should include all details; concision means that logistics documents should avoid using **redundant** words and expressions. In order to avoid unnecessary **delays** or misunderstandings, logistics documents should be prepared in time.[4]

Trade between two companies located in different countries begins with the business contract. Physical moment of the goods must be linked with the movement of various related documents. In actual practice, the logistics documents are very important in the international trade.

【Key Words】

formatted [ˈfɔːmætid]	adj.	有格式的
generator [ˈdʒenəreitə(r)]	n.	发电机, 发生器; 生产者, 创始者
instantly [ˈinstəntli]	adv.	立即地, 即刻地; 立即, 马上
eliminate [iˈlimineit]	v.	排除, 剔除; 淘汰, 消灭
indispensable [ˌindiˈspensəbl]	adj.	不可缺少的
multimodal [mʌltiˈmɔudl]	adj.	多种方式的, 多种模式的

characteristic [ˌkærəktəˈristik]	n.	特点，特征；品质
integrated [ˈintigreitid]	adj.	整体的，完整的
consistent [kənˈsistənt]	adj.	始终如一的；一致的，连贯的
ambiguous [æmˈbigjuəs]	adj.	模棱两可的；不明确的
integrity [inˈtegrəti]	n.	诚实，正直；完整，完善
redundant [riˈdʌndənt]	adj.	多余的；冗长的
delay [diˈlei]	n.	耽搁；迟滞，延期

【Notes to Text A】

[1] For example, an easy-to-use online bill of lading generator will save time and provide the documents instantly.

easy-to-use 使用方便
generator 发电器，发生器

[2] It can reduce the cycle time for forwarding and presentation of documents. The exporter gets paid more quickly and the importer gets title to the goods sooner.

"for forwarding and presentation of the documents" 意为 "单据的传递和交付"，用 "for" 引导的介词短语作定语修饰 "the cycle time"。

"title to the goods" 意为 "货物的所有权"，类似的短语还有 "the key to the door" "the solution to the problem" "the ticket to the concert" "the invitation to the party" 等。

[3] Accuracy means that the details of logistics documents must be fully consistent with that of sales contract, ambiguous words and expressions can't be used.

"must be fully consistent with that of sales contract" 中的 "that" 指代的是 "the details"。

[4] In order to avoid unnecessary delays or misunderstandings, logistics documents should be prepared in time.

in order to 为了

"misunderstanding" 是动名词，意为 "误解"。"mis" 是表示 "坏，错误，否定" 的前缀，通常用在元音之前。

【Exercises to Text A】

I. Fill in the blanks.

1. In the modern world, _____ can be used to create, view, e-mail, and print the formatted document.

2. The electronic delivery of the bill of lading can _____ the trade finance process.

3. _____ are indispensable in the logistics services, which mainly include letter of credit, bill of lading, multimodal transport documents, invoice, etc. .

4. The major characteristics about documents are _____.

5. _____ means that the details of logistics documents must be fully consistent with that of sales contract, ambiguous words and expressions can't be used.

II. Choose the best answer.

1. The electronic delivery of the bill of lading can (   ) the trade finance process.
   A. slow down   B. retard
   C. obstruct   D. speed up
2. _____ gets paid more quickly and _____ gets title to the goods sooner. (   )
   A. The exporter; the importer   B. The importer; the exporter
   C. The importer; the buyer   D. The exporter; the seller
3. The major characteristics about documents are (   ), integrated, concise and timely.
   A. large   B. small
   C. accurate   D. short

III. True or false.

1. The electronic delivery of the bill of lading can reduce the cycle time for forwarding and presentation of documents.   (   )
2. Logistics documents are dispensable in the logistics services.   (   )
3. In order to avoid unnecessary delays or misunderstandings, logistics documents should be prepared in time.   (   )

IV. Translation.

1. 出口方可以更快地得到付款，进口方可以更快地取得货物的所有权。

2. 在物流服务中，物流单据是必不可少的。

3. 为了避免不必要的延迟或误解，物流单据应该及时准备好。

Letter of Credit

1. Concept of L/C

A letter of credit is a written promise which is issued to the exporter by the opening or **issuing bank** upon the request of the importer, promising a certain payment to a **beneficiary** against complying documents as stated in the letter of credit.[1] Letter of credit is **abbreviated** as LC or L/C, and often is referred to as a documentary credit, abbreviated as DC or D/C.

When reading a letter of credit, we can find the main content of L/C includes the follow information: issuing bank, type of documentary credit, date and place of issue, date and place of expiry, applicant, beneficiary, advising bank, documents required, description of goods or services, and so on.

2. Type of L/C

Letter of credit may be either revocable or irrevocable. Either a L/C is **revocable** or is irrevocable, it is referenced on its face.

A revocable letter of credit may be **revoked** or modified for any reason, at any time by the issuing bank without notification.[2] If a **correspondent** bank is engaged in a transaction that involves a revocable letter of credit, it serves as the advising bank. It is not a commonly used instrument, and is generally used to provide guidelines for shipment.

The irrevocable letter of credit may not be revoked or amended without the agreement of the issuing bank, the advising bank, and the beneficiary. An irrevocable letter of credit insures the beneficiary that if the required documents are presented and the terms and conditions are complied with, payment will be made.[3]

3. The Operation of Documentary Credit

First, the issuance of a L/C starts with the buyer who instructs his bank to open a L/C in favor of the seller for the amount of the purchase. Then, the buyer's bank (issuing bank) sends the L/C to its correspondent in the seller's country, the negotiating bank or the advising bank, giving instructions about the amount of the credit, the beneficiary, the currency, the documents required and other special instructions. Upon receipt of the L/C, the correspondent advises the seller of the same immediately. The seller deals with the correspondent bank and prepares for the shipment of the buyer's order. After shipment, the seller presents the relative shipment documents to the correspondent bank. Then, the correspondent bank pays the money to the seller when documents presented are found to be in order, and then sends all the shipping documents to the buyer's bank, which, in turn, passes them to the buyer, who finally **reimburses** the correspondent bank through the buyer's bank.

4. Advantages of Using L/C under Documentary Credit

As the documentary credit is operated though banks, so it has advantages to both the applicant and beneficiary.[4] For the applicant, it is a conditional **undertaking** where payment can be made on his behalf only against the documents which will transfer to him the title to the goods. For the beneficiary, it is a bank undertaking to which he can look for payment. Besides, the L/C improves credit and negotiating status of the importer, so the importer may be able to negotiate for a lower purchase price and better terms.

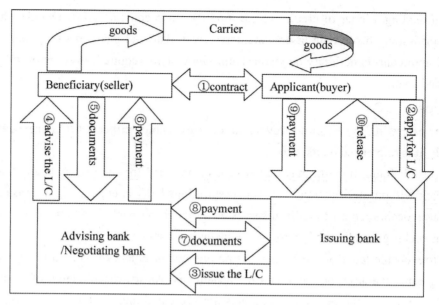

Figure 10.1 Using L/C under documentary credit

5. Negotiability Characteristic of L/C

Letter of credit are usually **negotiable**. The issuing bank is obligated to pay not only the beneficiary, but also any bank **nominated** by the beneficiary. Negotiable instruments are passed freely from one party to another almost in the same way as money. To be negotiable, the letter of credit must include an unconditional promise to pay, on demand or at a **definite** time.

The nominated bank becomes a holder **in due course**. As a holder in due course, the holder takes the letter of credit for **authority**, in **good faith**, without notice of any claims against it. The transaction is considered a straight negotiation if the issuing bank's payment obligation extends also to the beneficiary of the credit. If a L/C is a straight negotiation it is referenced on its face by "we **engage with** you" or "available with ourselves".

6. Discrepancies

A most important point for the exporter to remember is that the documents, which are an integral part of the documentary credit, must be absolutely in accord with those stipulated in the letter of credit. If there is any **discrepancy**, the undertaking of payment given by the bank no longer exists. Examples of common discrepancies are:

(1) The term of the letter of credit has expired.

(2) Shipment of goods is late.

(3) Inadequate in cover.

(4) Absence of a document.

Exporters should be most **vigilant** to ensure that they comply exactly with the stipulated documents required. If there are some requirements in the documentary credit that the exporter can not meet, he should seek to have it amended by the importer. Otherwise payment may not be received despite goods having been shipped. In practice, discrepancies can usually be overcome with the agreement of the importer but if, for example, the importer was seeking an excuse not to pay a discrepancy presents him with a ready opportunity to avoid payment.

【Key Words】

issuing bank		开证行
beneficiary [ˌbeniˈfiʃəri]	n.	受益人
abbreviate [əˈbriːvieit]	v.	缩写，使……简略
revocable [ˈrevəkəbl]	adj.	可废止的，可撤销的
revoke [riˈvəuk]	v.	撤回（回想）；取消；废除
correspondent [ˌkɔrəˈspɔndənt]	n.	记者，通讯员
reimburse [ˌriːimˈbɜːs]	vt.	偿还，报销；归还
undertake [ˌʌndəˈteik]	v.	承担；承诺
negotiable [niˈɡəuʃjəbl]	adj.	可磋商的，可转让的；可流通的
nominate [ˈnɔmineit]	v.	任命；挑选；指定
definite [ˈdefinət]	adj.	明确的；不会改变的
in due course		顺次
authority [ɔːˈθɔrəti]	n.	权力；权威人士，专家；许可
good faith		真诚；善意
engage with		与……接洽；与……衔接
discrepancy [disˈkrepənsi]	n.	差异，不一致
vigilant [ˈvidʒilənt]	adj.	警醒的，警惕的；警戒的

【Notes to Text B】

[1] A letter of credit is a written promise which is issued to the exporter by the opening or issuing bank upon the request of (the applicant) the importer, promising a certain payment to a beneficiary (the exporter) against the appropriate documents as stated in the letter of credit.

"which"引导的定语从句用来解释说明"letter of credit"是怎么样的一种书面保证；"promising"引领的现在分词短语作状语，对信用证的定义进行补充说明。

[2] A revocable letter of credit may be revoked or modified for any reason, at any time by the issuing bank without notification.

"without"在此处作介词，意为"无，没有"。例如：
Without the sun, nothing would grow. 没有太阳，就不会有生物。
The rumor was without foundation. 那条谣言毫无根据。"without notification"是指"无须通知"。
a revocable letter of credit 可撤销信用证

[3] An irrevocable letter of credit insures the beneficiary that if the required documents are presented and the terms and conditions are complied with, payment will be made.

"present"此处意为"提交,呈现",如"present the report""present the plan"。

"complied with"意为"照……行事,答应"。例如:

Everyone should comply with the law. 每个人都应该遵守法律。

"the conditions are complied with"这里省略了"the stipulation of L/C",即单证一致。

[4] As the documentary credit is operated through banks, so it has advantages to both the applicant and beneficiary.

documentary credit   跟单信用证

这里的"bank"指的是"issuing bank"和"negotiation bank"。

【Exercises to Text B】

I. Fill in the blanks.

1. A letter of credit is a written promise which is issued to the exporter by _____.
2. As the documentary credit is operated though banks, so it has advantages to _____.
3. _____ is obligated to pay not only the beneficiary, but also any bank nominated by the beneficiary.
4. To be negotiable, the letter of credit must include _____ to pay, on demand or at a definite time.
5. The nominated bank becomes _____ in due course.

II. Choose the best answer.

1. A letter of credit is a written promise which is issued to _____ by the opening or issuing bank upon the request of _____. ( )

   A. the exporter; the importer   B. the importer; the exporter
   C. the importer; the buyer   D. the exporter; the seller

2. For the applicant, it is a conditional undertaking where payment can be made on his behalf only against the (   ).

   A. documents   B. goods
   C. title   D. payment

3. The L/C improves credit and negotiating status of the importer, so the importer may be able to negotiate for a (   ) purchase price and better terms.

   A. higher   B. steady
   C. lower   D. unquiet

4. The transaction is considered a straight negotiation if the (   ) payment obligation extends also to the beneficiary of the credit.

   A. seller's   B. exporter's
   C. issuing bank's   D. buyer's

III. True or false.

1. Letter of credit is abbreviated as LC or L/C, and often is referred to as a documentary credit, abbreviated as DC or D/C.   (   )
2. Either an L/C is revocable or is irrevocable, it is referenced on its back.   (   )
3. Besides, the L/C improves credit and negotiating status of the importer.   (   )

4. To be negotiable, the letter of credit must include the conditional promise to pay, on demand or at a definite time.   (   )

IV. Translation.

1. 信用证是基于申请者（进口方）的请求，由开证银行开给出口方的一份书面保证，如果有信用证所列的适当单据，就保证给受益人（出口方）一定数额的支付款。

2. 可撤销的信用证可以由开证行在没有通知的情况下，在任意时间因任何原因撤销或修改。

3. 如果出示了所要求的单据，并且与贸易术语和各项条件一致，不可撤销信用证能够确保受益人得到付款。

4. 信用证能够提高进口方信贷和议付的条件，从而也能以更低的购买价格和更优惠的条件来议付。

Bill of Lading

1. Concept of Bill of Lading (B/L)

A bill of lading is a document issued and signed by a **shipping company** or its agents **acknowledging** that the goods mentioned in the bill of lading have been duly received for shipment, or shipped on board of a vessel, and undertaking to deliver the goods in the like order and condition as received, to the consignee.

2. Functions of B/L

Marine bill of lading perform a number of functions. Generally, it is **receipt for the goods shipped**, a **document of title** to the goods and evidence of the terms of the contract of a consignment.[1]

A bill of lading is a receipt issued by a carrier that an identifiable consignment of goods has been received by him for shipment, or actually loaded on board his ship. The bill of lading as a receipt will show the quantity and condition of the cargo loaded, ship's name, the destination, details of date and so on.

A bill of lading is a document of title to the goods. The **possession** of a bill of lading is **equivalent** in law to possession of the goods. The holder of the bill of lading is able to obtain delivery of the goods at the port of destination and during transit the goods can be sold merely by endorsing the bill of lading.

Additionally, the terms of bill of lading provide evidence of the contract of carriage between the carrier and the shipper. The terms of the bill of lading contain the terms of the contract.

3. Types of B/L

There are several types of bill of lading, and some of them can be discussed as following:

(1) **Order B/L** versus **Straight B/L**. Order B/L means that the carrier will deliver the goods at the port of destination not solely to the named consignee, but to any person **designated** by him. An order B/L is a negotiable document. However, straight B/L is not negotiable, and can't be transferred to the third parties, so delivery of goods can only be taken by the named consignee.[2]

(2) **On board shipped B/L** versus **Received for shipment B/L**. The former confirms that the goods have been loaded and are actually on board of the ship. However, the later is issued by the shipping company when goods have been given into the **custody** of the shipping company, but have not yet been placed on board of the vessel.

(3) **Clean B/L** versus **Unclean B/L**. The clean B/L indicates that the goods were received without damages, **irregularities** or short shipment, there was no **defect** in the apparent order and condition of the goods at the time of receipt or shipment. In contrast, the unclean B/L, which is also called dirty B/L or claused B/L, is the opposite of the clean B/L, usually the words "**insufficient packing**", "missing safety seal" or the like are indicated on the B/L.[3]

(4) **Direct B/L** versus **Through B/L**. The direct B/L means that the cargo is always on the same ship from port of lading to port of destination. In other words, transshipment hasn't happened. However, the through B/L covers goods being transshipped during the transportation, but the first carrier has the responsibility as the principal carrier for all stages of the journey.

(1) SHIPPER		(10) B/L NO.
(2) CONSIGNEE		COSCO 中国远洋运输（集团）总公司 CHINA OCEANSHIPPING (GROUP) CO. ORIGINAL COMBINED TRANPORT BILL OF LADING
(3) NOTIFY PARTY		
(4) PLACE OF RECEIPT	(5) OCEAN VESSEL	
(6) VOYAGE NO.	(7) PORT OF LOADING	
(8) PORT OF DISCHARGE	(9) PLACE OF DELIVERY	

Continued

(11) MARKS (12) NOS & KINDS OF PKGS (13) DESCRIPTION OF GOODS (14) G. W. (kg) (15) MEAS(m^3)					
(16) TOTAL NUMBER OF CONTAINERS OR PACKAGES(IN WORDS)					
FREIGHT & CHARGES	REVENUE TONS	RATE	PER	PREPAID	COLLECT
PREPAID AT	PAYABLE AT		(17) PLACE AND DATE OF ISSUE		
TOTAL PREPAID	(18) NUMBER OF ORIGINAL B(S)L				
LOADING ON BOARD THE VESSEL (19) DATE			(20) BY		

Figure 10.2 Sample of bill of lading

Besides the above several kinds of bill of ladings, types of marine B/L are also include the long form B/L and the short form B/L, etc. .

4. Issuing Bill of Lading

The bill of lading should be signed by either shipping company or an authorized agent, and it must show how many signed originals were issued. The originals, which are marked as "originals" on their face, are proof of ownership of goods.[4] Bill of lading is made out in sets and any number of copies may constitute the set according to the requirements of the particular transaction and the importer. A set contains at least two originals. Usually, a set of three originals is the most common.

5. Date of Bill of Lading

The date of bill of lading is very important, if the letter of credit stipulates a deadline for shipment. Because the B/L can show whether the goods have been shipped on time. Unless otherwise specified in the credit document or unless the insurance document clearly specifies that the cover is effective at the latest from the date of shipment, the insurance document must be dated not later than the date of issuing of the bill of lading.

6. Endorsement on Bill of Lading

In practice, some bill of ladings can be transferable. The consigner or consignee can transfer the B/L by **endorsement**. There are two kinds of endorsement: **special endorsement** and **endorsement in blank**.[5] The holder may **convert** the blank endorsement **into** a special endorsement by inserting the name of a person to whom delivery is to be made.

【Key Words】

shipping company		船运公司
acknowledge [ək'nɔlidʒ]	v.	承认；接受，告知收到
receipt for the goods		货物收据
document of title		物权凭证
possession [pə'zeʃ(ə)n]	n.	财产，所有；占有
equivalent [i'kwivələnt]	adj.	等价的；相等的
	n.	等价物；等同物
order B/L		指示提单
straight B/L		记名提单
designate ['dezigneit]	v.	指定；标示；指派，委任
on board shipped B/L		已装船提单
received for shipment B/L		收货待运提单
custody ['kʌstədi]	n.	保管；拘留，监禁
clean B/L		清洁提单
unclean B/L		不清洁提单
irregularity [i,regjə'lærəti]	n.	不规则；非正式；不整齐
defect [di'fekt]	n.	缺点；瑕疵
insufficient packing		包装不良
direct B/L		直达提单
through B/L		联运提单
endorsement [in'dɔːsmənt]	n.	支持，赞同；背书
special endorsement		特别背书
endorsement in blank		空白背书
convert…into…		把……转变成……

【Notes to Text C】

[1] Generally, it is receipt for the goods shipped, a document of title to the goods and evidence of the terms of the contract of a consignment.

"shipped" 是过去分词充当后置定语修饰 "goods"。

the terms of the contract of a consignment   货物合同条款

[2] However, straight B/L is not negotiable, and can't be transferred to the third parties, so delivery of goods can only be taken by the named consignee.

straight B/L   记名提单   指的是提单必须有指定的收货人提货，不能转让第三方。

take delivery of...   接收，提取   此句中，"delivery of goods can only be taken by..." 意为 "货物只能由……提取"。

named consignee   指定的提货人

[3] In contrast, the unclean B/L, which is also called dirty B/L or claused B/L, is the opposite of the

clean B/L, usually the words "insufficient packing", "missing safety seal" or the like are indicated on the B/L.

"in contrast" 与此相反，例如：In contrast with our system, theirs seems very old-fashioned. 他们的制度与我们的相比，显得过于守旧了。这里突出了"clean B/L"和"unclean B/L"的差别。

"opposite" 此处作名词，意为"对立物，对立者，对手，对立面"，例如：Black and white are opposites. 黑和白相反。"opposite" 还可以作形容词，意为"对立的，相反的"，如"opposite effect" "opposite direction"。

[4] The originals, which are marked as "originals" on their face, are proof of ownership of goods.

"original" 此处作名词，意为"原件，原稿"。"original" 还可以作形容词，意为"最初的，原始的，原版的"，例如：The original picture is in the British Museum. 这幅画的原作在大英博物馆内。

on their face 在单据的表面

[5] There are two kinds of endorsement: special endorsement and endorsement in blank.

special endorsement 特别背书，又称记名背书。在票据背面记明被背书人的姓名或公司、背书年月日及背书人的签名。被背书人是因背书而取得票据权利的人，其资格法律一般不加限制。

endorsement in blank 空白背书，又称无记名背书、略式背书、不完全背书，是指不记载被背书人名称而仅由背书人签章的背书，票据可以被自由转让。

【Exercises to Text C】

I. Fill in the blanks.

1. A bill of lading is a receipt issued by a carrier that an identifiable consignment of goods has been _____, or actually loaded on board his ship.

2. Additionally, the terms of bill of lading provide _____ between the carrier and the shipper.

3. Order B/L means that the carrier will deliver the goods at the port of destination not solely to the named consignee, but to _____.

4. In contrast, the unclean B/L, which is also called dirty B/L or claused B/L, is the opposite of the _____.

5. The consigner or consignee can transfer the B/L by _____.

II. Choose the best answer.

1. Which of the following is not the function of bill of lading? (   )

    A. receipt for the goods shipped

    B. a document of title to the goods

    C. evidence of the contract of a consignment

    D. the contract of a consignment

2. (   ) means that the carrier will deliver the goods at the port of destination not solely to the named consignee, but to any person designated by him.

    A. Order B/L   B. Packing List

    C. Shipper Order   D. Manifest

3. The (   ) means that the cargo is always on the same ship from port of lading to port of destination.

    A. though B/L   B. clean B/L

C. direct B/L   D. order B/L
4. A set contains at least (　) originals.
   A. one   B. two
   C. three   D. ten
5. A (　) is issued by the shipper to the carrier requesting allocation of shipping space.
   A. B/L   B. insurance policy
   C. shipping note   D. manifest

III. True or false.

1. A bill of lading is a document issued and signed by a shipper.　　　　　　　　　(　)
2. Marine bill of lading is exactly the contract of carriage.　　　　　　　　　　　(　)
3. An order B/L is a negotiable document. However, straight B/L is not negotiable, and can be transferred to the third parties.　　　　　　　　　　　　　　　　　　　　　　　(　)
4. The clean B/L indicates that the goods were received without damages, irregularities or short shipment.　　　　　　　　　　　　　　　　　　　　　　　　　　　　　　　　(　)
5. The consigner or consignee can transfer the B/L by endorsement.　　　　　　　(　)

IV. Translation.

1. 海运提单是由船运公司或其代理人签发的，表明单据中所提到的货物已经收到待运或已经装到船只的甲板上，并且把货物以收到的次序和状态交付给收货人。

2. 海运提单的条款提供了对承运人和托运人之间运输合同的证明。

3. 指示提单意味着承运人在目的港不仅可以把货物交付给指定姓名的收货人，还可以交给由其指定的任意人。

4. 与此相反，不清洁提单，也被称为肮脏提单或附有条件的提单，与清洁提单是相对的，通常提单上有"包装不良""安全的印章或封条丢失"等类似字样。

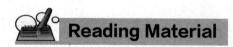

Logistics Documents in Practice

Invoice is bill for goods and **sets forth** the terms of sale. The invoice is also a basic document. It must fully **identify** the overseas shipment and serve as a basis for the preparation of all other documents which **reproduce** information from it.

Insurance policy provides protection to cargo owners in the event of loss or damage to cargo in transit. There are different types of insurance policies for different **categories** of risks to be covered.

Packing list may be shown on invoice or **separately**, and should contain item by item, the contents of containers with its weight and description.

The **certificate of origin** certifies that place of the origin of the merchandise. Besides the **Federation of Chambers of Commerce**, various other **trade associations** have been authorizes by government to issue certificates of origin.

The bill of lading is not a contract of carriage as it is signed only by the carrier. However, it provides evidence of contract of carriage. It serves as a receipt for goods delivered to the carrier, and as a document of title enabling the goods to be transferred from the shipper to the consignee or any other party by endorsement.

A seaway bill is the **replacement** of the traditional ocean bill of lading. The sea way bill is a non-negotiable document and made out to a named consignee who is allowed, upon production of proper identification, to claim the goods without presenting the waybill.

The airway bill is the important document for a **batch** of air freight goods. It constitutes evidence of the **conclusion** of the contract of freight, and the evidence of receipt of goods and conditions of carriage.

A **cargo manifest** provides information regarding cargo on board. A freight manifest gives information regarding freight rates, **surcharges**, **rebates**, etc.. The manifest is prepared by the carrier's agent but the freight forwarder has to handle it while dealing with the customs and port authorities.

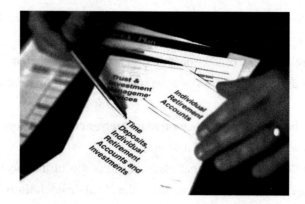

A **shipping note** is issued by the shipper to the carrier requesting allocation of shipping space. It is a commitment on the part of the shipper to ship the goods and serves as the basis for the preparation of the bill of lading.

A **delivery order** is issued by the carrier or his agent to enable the consignee or his forwarding agent to take delivery of the cargo from the vessel.

A **mate's receipt**, which is subsequently exchanged for the bill of lading, is the receipt issued by the carrier in the acknowledgement of the goods on board. When the cargo is loaded on the ship, the commanding officer of the ship will issue a receipt called the mate's receipt for goods.

Dock receipt is a receipt that may be issued by a port authority to confirm receipt of the goods on the quay or warehouse before shipment. The dock receipt is used to transfer responsibility when an export item is moved by the domestic carrier to the port of embarkation and left with the international carrier for movement to its final destination.

A **weight certificate** confirms that the goods are in line with the weight specified on the bill of lading, invoice, insurance certificate or other specified documents. In so doing, it confirms to the buyer, seller, insurance or other specified parties that the goods were at a specified weight at the time of shipment. The weight certificate is usually requested by the importer to confirm that the weight of the goods is in conformity with the exporter sales contract at the time of shipment.

Quality certificate confirms that the quality and specification of a particular consignment of goods is in conformity with the sales contract at the time of shipment. It may be issued by the exporter or a relevant government department as required under letter of credit or sales contract terms. It is essential that cargo description in the quality certificate conform to its terms found in other relevant documents, such as commercial invoice, letter of credit, insurance policy, etc..

【Key Words】

set forth   陈述（出发，宣布）

Chapter 10　Logistics Documents

identify [ai'dentifai]	v.	识别，认出；鉴定，确定
reproduce [ˌriːprə'djuːs]	v.	再生，复制；生殖
insurance policy		保险单
category ['kætəgəri]	n.	种类，类别
separately ['sepərətli]	adv.	分别地；单独地
certificate of origin		原产地证书
Federation of Chambers of Commerce		商品贸易委员会
trade association		同业公会；贸易协会
replacement [ri'pleismənt]	n.	交换，更换；替代者，替代品
batch [bætʃ]	n.	一批，一组；成批，分批
conclusion [kən'kluːʒn]	n.	结论，结束；签订
cargo manifest		货物舱单
surcharge ['sɜːtʃɑːdʒ]	n.	超载，额外费用；附加费
rebate ['riːbeit]	n.	减少；折扣，回扣
shipping note		托运单；船货清单，装货通知单
delivery order		交货单
mate's receipt		大副收据
dock receipt		码头收据
weight certificate		重量证书
quality certificate		质量证书

【Questions】

1. How many documents can you enumerate after reading this article?
2. Please discuss the three documents—bill of lading, seaway bill and airway bill.
3. What is shipping note?
4. What function does the delivery order have?

Chapter 11
International Logistics

A Reliable Partner of P&G[①] on International Logistics

While preparing for a major market **launch** and **penetration** in the U.S., the world's largest consumer product company, P&G, turned to R+L Global Logistics for an international logistics solution.

【参考音频】

---

① P&G P&G是Procter & Gamble 的简称，是一家日用消费品公司，其产品包括洗发、护肤、化妆、婴幼儿护理用品等。

Chapter 11 International Logistics

1. Problem

During the planning phase, P&G discovered that its traditional ocean-based transportation and logistics model could not meet time-critical deadlines. To avoid **outages** on the retailers' shelves, the company needed reliable solutions from a transportation and logistics company with a history of crafting international logistics solutions.

Ensuring that the products arrived in the stores well ahead of the launch date was absolutely essential for marketing success. In addition to the time **constraints**, the goods would have to be moved efficiently from the Far East to the U.S. and be successfully put into the distribution supply chain without interruption.

In order to resolve the problem, P&G identified five critical requirements of a new logistics provider:

(1) A proven track record of on-time delivery.

(2) A full **complement** of international and domestic logistics services.

(3) A knowledge of product launch for major retail promotions.

(4) Leading edge automation and technology for tracing and tracking shipments.

(5) A sound **reputation** for crafting reliable and flexible logistics solutions in time-critical settings.

2. Solution

As time was running out, P&G turned to one of its minority-owned suppliers, R+L Global Logistics, for help.

Working closely together, the two companies were able to craft a workable solution and deploy the resources necessary to move the goods to the required destinations ahead of the deadlines.

A critical success factor was R+L Global's ability to identify and secure **a fleet of** Boeing 747 freighters, which were chartered to transport the goods from the Far East to the U.S. R+L Global's experience in international shipping enabled them to quickly satisfy the charter requirements by identifying the right airline with the right schedule, at the right price.

Another essential advantage was R+L Global's ability to coordinate directly with the supplier to receive the goods. R+L Global arranged to have the airline pallets built in **compliance** with aircraft **contours** and specifications, and tendered them directly to the Charter operator in order to **expedite** the process.

Upon arrival in the U.S., R+L Global was responsible for the recovery of the airline pallets, breaking them down, and rebuilding the thousands of loose cartons onto Chep™[①] pallets in order to comply with the customer's **stringent** distribution requirements.

The entire process from the original airport to the client's distribution center was completed in two days.

【Outline】

Working in close partnership with the customer, manufacturer, global partners, and airlines, R+L Global was able to meet each of the time-critical deadlines. All of the products were delivered intact and on time for a successful market launch. R+L Global Logistics was rewarded with a "valuable supplier" status by the customer and afforded new opportunities to expand their offerings.

【Key Words】

launch [lɔːntʃ]	v.	发射；开展（活动、计划等）；发动，发起；上市
	n.	发射；发起；上市
penetration [ˌpeniˈtreiʃn]	n.	渗透；穿透；洞察力
outage [ˈaʊtidʒ]	n.	断供期；断供
constraint [kənˈstreint]	n.	约束，限制；克制
complement [ˈkɔmpliment]	n.	补充；补语；补充物；足额
	vt.	补充；补助；衬托
reputation [ˌrepjuˈteiʃn]	n.	名气，名誉
fleet [fliːt]	n.	舰队，船队；车队
a fleet of		一队
compliance [kəmˈplaiəns]	n.	服从；遵守
contour [ˈkɔntʊər]	n.	外形，轮廓；（地图）等高线；概要
expedite [ˈekspədait]	vt.	加快进展；迅速完成
stringent [ˈstrindʒənt]	adj.	严格的；迫切的；（货币）紧缩的

---

① Chep™ Chep是一家在世界范围内提供托盘与周转箱共用服务的领导公司，在几十个国家拥有数百个服务中心。

Chapter 11　International Logistics

Text A

Concepts of International Logistics

As an emerging industry, international logistics **associated** with the development of international trade has become increasingly broad prospects.[1] Huge array of shippers, carriers, forwarders, businessmen, and so on **facilitate** international transactions, trades, and movement of goods and services. Thereby, international logistics management is facing enormous challenges. The cost of logistics as a percentage of total cost is greater for international ventures, and the complexity of logistics usually increases at a **geometric** rate in the international **arena**.[2]

International logistics—the movement of goods across national boundaries—occurs in the following situations:[3]

(1) A firm exports a portion of a product made or grown, for example, papermaking machinery to Sweden, wheat to Russia, or coal to Japan.

(2) A firm imports raw materials such as **pulpwood** from Canada, or manufactured products such as motorcycles from Japan.

(3) A firm is global in outlook and sees almost all nations as being markets, sources of supply, or sites of assembly operations.

(4) Because of geography, cargo has to be transported through the third country on the way from the export nation to the import nation. Sometimes they are temporarily deposited in the third country, or sometimes they directly cross the borders. Then the cargo remains the fundamental conditions to the import nation. For example, when an inland country is planning to deal with countries which are not **adjacent**, he has to consider the movement of goods crossing his neighbors' borders.[4]

To create customer satisfaction, unnecessary costs must be lowered and efficiency must be increased throughout the trade process. So organizations strive to focus on core competencies and are becoming more flexible. More and more companies choose to **outsource** logistics aspect by partnering with a third party logistics provider, which can perform the activities better or more cost effectively.[5]

For example, an international **freight forwarder** is an agent who typically arranges cargo movement to an overseas destination. They are capable to **consolidate** and **assemble** small shipments into full loads and then **disperse** them after transport to the point of consumption. This type of companies have **expertise** that allows them to prepare and process the documentation and perform related activities such as space booking, packaging, international insurance, and customs clearance. Although a freight forwarder often acts only as an agent, not as a carrier, it provides nearly all of the services that are important to international trade operations.[6] Whether an exporter /importer is large or small, the weight of the cargo is light or heavy, a freight forwarder can take care of the cargo from "dock to door", thus freeing the shippers from dealing with the multitude of logistics-related details.

【Key Words】

associate [əˈsəuʃieit]	v.	（使）发生联系；（使）联合；与……交往
	n.	伙伴，同事；合伙人
	adj.	准的，副的；联合的，有关联的
facilitate [fəˈsiliteit]	vt.	使便利；促进，促使
geometric [ˌdʒiəˈmetrik]	adj.	几何学的，几何图案的；成几何级数增加的
arena [əˈriːnə]	n.	表演场地，竞技场；活动领域
pulpwood [ˈpʌlpwud]	n.	纸浆用木材
adjacent [əˈdʒeisənt]	adj.	毗邻的，邻近的
outsource [ˈautsɔːs]	vt.	外购；外包（工程）
freight [freit]	n.	货运，货物；运费；航运货物；货运列车
	vt.	运输；装货于
forwarder [ˈfɔːwədə]	n.	代运人；运输业者；转运公司
consolidate [kənˈsɔlideit]	v.	巩固，加强；（使）合并，（使）结成一体
assemble [əˈsembl]	v.	聚集，收集；组装
disperse [disˈpɜːs]	v.	（使）分散，疏散；散播，传播
expertise [ˌekspɜːˈtiːz]	n.	专门知识或技术；专长

【Notes to Text A】

[1] As an emerging industry, international logistics associated with the development of international trade has become increasingly broad prospects.

此处"as"是一个介词，意为"作为"。例如：

Chapter 11　International Logistics

As a teacher, I am very aware of the characteristics of post-90 students. 作为一名教师，我非常清楚"90后"学生的特点。

"associated with the development of international trade"是定语，修饰前面的主语"international logistics"，整个句子的谓语是"has become"。"be associated with"意为"和……联系在一起""与……有关"。

[2] The cost of logistics as a percentage of total cost is greater for international ventures, and the complexity of logistics usually increases at a geometric rate in the international arena.

"as"引导的介词短语作定语，意为"作为总成本的一部分"，修饰前面的"the cost"。

"geometric"意为"成几何级数增加的"，例如：Population is increasing in that country at a geometric progression. 那个国家的人口正以几何级数增长。

[3] International logistics—the movement of goods across national boundaries—occurs in the following situations:

"the movement of goods across national boundaries"在此处作"international logistics"的同位语，起到解释的作用，并用短横线和前面的主语"international logistics"及后面的谓语"occur"联系。

[4] For example, when an inland country is planning to deal with countries which are not adjacent, he has to consider the movement of goods crossing his neighbors' borders.

"inland country"意为"内陆国"，也可写作"landlocked state"，指没有海岸线的国家，也即被周围邻国陆地领土所包围因而没有出海口的国家，又称陆锁国。

[5] More and more companies choose to outsource logistics aspect by partnering with a third party logistics provider, which can perform the activities better or more cost effectively.

"outsource"是及物动词，意为"外包"，其名词形式为"outsourcing"。外包业是新近兴起的一个行业，企业为维持组织竞争核心能力，将组织的非核心业务委托给外部的专业公司，以降低营运成本，它给企业带来了新的活力。外包有很多种形式，物流外包只是其中一种。

"which can perform the activities better or more cost effectively"作"which"引导的定语从句，修饰前面的"a Third-party Logistics provider"。

[6] Although a freight forwarder often acts only as an agent, not as a carrier, it provides nearly all of the services that are important to international trade operations.

"although"意思相当于"though"（尽管，虽然），用来引导让步状语从句，它所引导的从句不能和并列连词"but""and""so"等连用，但可以和"yet""still"等词连用。

"it"指的是"a freight forwarder"。

"that are important to international trade operations"是由"that"引导的定语从句，修饰前面的"the services"。

【Exercises to Text A】

I. Fill in the blanks.

1. As an emerging industry, international logistics _____ with the development of international trade has become increasingly broad prospects.

2. Huge array of shippers, carriers, forwarders, businessmen, and so on _____ international transactions, trades, and movement of goods and services.

3. More and more companies choose to _____ logistics aspect by partnering with a third-party logistics provider.

II. True or false.

1. The cost of logistics as a percentage of total cost is greater for international ventures.   (　)
2. Organizations strive to focus on core competencies and are becoming more flexible, so they all choose to outsource logistics aspect.   (　)
3. A freight forwarder acts only as an agent, not as a carrier.   (　)

III. Translation.

1. 作为一项新兴产业，国际物流是伴随着国际贸易的发展而发展起来的。

2. 国际物流管理面临着巨大的挑战。

3. 国际货运代理是一种主要负责安排货物的运输到达国外目的地的业务。

4. 货运代理使得托运人从处理大量与物流有关的细节中解脱出来。

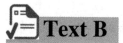 **Text B**

The Factors That Influence International Logistics

Extending logistics activities beyond a country's borders represents something more to a company than lengthening its transport distances.[1] International logistics is more difficult than domestic logistics, many factors influence the flow of goods among countries.

Political situations are very important. Friendly countries **negotiate** treaties to increase the flow of business among them. On the other hand, wars and **terrorism** have a **dampening** effect. For example, Iraq War put too much pressure on the world airline industry.

Economic conditions also influence trade patterns. The **devastating** effect of the 2008—2009 world financial crisis has been hard felt in the logistics industry. Global logistics volumes fell dramatically and the financial stability of many large carriers became questionable. Ocean carriers cut significant capacities, airlines reduced flights and road transport carriers were forced to park their fleets in the hope that global trade would **rebound**.[2] The good news is that many experts are **forecasting** a very gradual recovery in logistics volumes now.

Chapter 11　International Logistics

The rapidly changing technology influences international logistics, in particular, the changes in computer hardware and software.[3] The significant price reduction for powerful computer equipments have helped bring about better inventory control, better equipment scheduling, more efficient rating of transportation movements, and so on. The technological changes in communications (such as satellite global positioning systems to maintain contact with motor carrier fleets) have helped to improve service quality to the extent that motor carrier companies are now able to meet narrowly defined time windows for pickups and deliveries.[4] They also speed up order processing, document flow and improve **accuracy**. The interface between communication technology and computers is another area that has tremendous potential for logistics. These items are just a tip of the iceberg; many other things could be included in this area, such as bar coding and robotics.

Environmental protection issues are also having an impact. Many nations are **enacting** more **stringent** packaging regulations in an effort to increase resource recycling.[5] Aircraft noise restrictions are forcing airlines to retire aircraft from some markets (although they still can be used in some parts of the world). In Europe, automobile manufacturers have to use an emission standard, from Euro I to Euro V, for their vehicles. The automobiles will not be launched to markets without going through professional detections. The norm contributes to a green environment by reducing harmful gases emissions.

Cultural differences play major roles in transactions. The German businessmen may be very direct and **precise** in price negotiations, whereas the Italian may be very hospitable, but not always **punctual**. Indeed everyone should thoroughly understand and respect different cultural background, religious beliefs, and moral concepts, if he wishes to success in international logistics.[6]

【Key Words】

negotiate [ni'gəuʃieit]	v.	谈判，协商；交涉；谈判达成；议价出售
terrorism ['terərizəm]	n.	恐怖主义，恐怖手段；恐怖状态
dampen ['dæmpən]	vt.	弄湿；抑制；减弱
devastating ['devəsteitiŋ]	adj.	毁灭性的；引人注目的；令人震惊的
rebound [ri'baund]	v.	弹回，反弹；产生反作用；使回升
	n.	反弹球；弹回，跳回；振作
forecast ['fɔːkɑːst]	vt.	预报，预测
	n.	预测，预报；预言
accuracy ['ækjərəsi]	n.	精确（性），精确程度，准确（性）
enact [i'nækt]	vt.	制定（法律），通过（法案）
stringent ['strindʒənt]	adj.	严格的，严厉的，（货币）紧缩的
precise [pri'sais]	adj.	精确的，准确的；正规的；精密的
punctual ['pʌŋktʃuəl]	adj.	守时的，准时的

【Notes to Text B】

[1] Extending logistics activities beyond a country's borders represents something more to a company than lengthening its transport distances.

"extending" 和 "lengthening" 都是 "动词原形 +ing" 构成的动名词。本句中 "extending logistics activities beyond a country's borders" 作主语，谓语是 "represent"，宾语是 "something more"。

"than" 构成比较级，注意其前后对比的结构要相似。

该句变成这种形式更易于理解：To a company, extending logistics activities beyond a country's borders represents something more than lengthening its transport distances.

[2] Ocean carriers cut significant capacities, airlines reduced flights and road transport carriers were forced to park their fleets in the hope that global trade would rebound.

"ocean carriers cut significant capacities" "airlines reduced flights and road transport" 及 "carriers were forced to park their fleets" 是 3 个并列的句子，意为 "海运企业大量削减运量、航空公司减少航班、陆运企业被迫停运车辆"。物流业的主要运输方式就是水运、空运和陆运。这些物流运输企业都大幅削减运力，意味着经济形势不容乐观。

"in the hope that global trade would rebound" 作状语，其中的 "that" 又引导了一个定语从句，修饰 "hope"。

[3] The rapidly changing technology influences international logistics, in particular, the changes in computer hardware and software.

"in particular" 相当于 "particularly"，意为 "尤其，特别"，表示语气或意思的进一步延伸或强化。例如：

The goals and scope, in particular, show you the direction to move. 特别是目标和范围能告诉您下一步工作的方向。

这句话在段首起到提示的作用，表示这段话介绍的是快速发展的技术因素对国际物流的影响。

[4] The technological changes in communications (such as satellite global positioning systems to

maintain contact with motor carrier fleets) have helped to improve service quality to the extent that motor carrier companies are now able meet narrowly defined time windows for pickups and deliveries.

maintain contact with 与……保持联系

"to the extent that motor carrier companies are now able to meet narrowly defined time windows for pickups and deliveries" 是一个由 "to the extent that" 引导的结果状语从句。

[5] Many nations are enacting more stringent packaging regulations in an effort to increase resource recycling.

"in an effort to" 意为 "为了达成，为了完成"。例如：

They rebuilt the cinemas in an effort to reach out to the young people. 他们重建了电影院以吸引年轻人。

[6] Indeed everyone should thoroughly understand and respect different cultural background, religious beliefs, and moral concepts, if he wishes to success in international logistics.

此句是一个倒装句，把 "if" 引导的从句放在句尾，意在强调 "了解和尊重不同的宗教信仰和道德观念"。

【Exercises to Text B】

I. Choose the best answer.

1. International logistics is defined as exporting and importing products (　　) the boundaries of a country.
   A. beyond   B. on
   C. in   D. of

2. Operating internationally creates different requirement than (　　).
   A. to operate domestic   B. operating domestical
   C. operating domestically   D. operating domesticable

3. In the 2008—2009 world financial crisis logistics companies all hoped that global trade would (　　).
   A. rebound   B. lengthen
   C. add   D. gain

4. Which does not belong to the application of information technology in international logistics activities? (　　)
   A. ERP   B. VMI
   C. RFID   D. GPS

5. Which factor would not cause cultural difference in international trade? (　　)
   A. religious beliefs   B. moral concepts
   C. language   D. writing instruments

II. Reading and answering questions.

Customer service is a vital component of international logistics management. Each activity of logistics management contributes to the level of service a company provides to its customers. However, transportation's impact on customer service is one of the most significant in international logistics.

There are four transportation modes: motor, rail, water, or pipeline. Certain model combinations are multimodal transportation, including rail-motor, motor-water, motor-air, and rail-water. Such inter-modal combination offer specialized services, with more flexibility, lower cost and so on, than a single transport mode. The third party logistics providers often apply this combination into customized international and domestic service.

Questions:

1. The prime aim of international logistics management is (   ).
   A. lower cost   B. the flow of information
   C. customer satisfy   D. greater efficiency
2. The advantage of multimodal transportation is (   ).
   A. size   B. flexibility
   C. varieties   D. volume
3. Multimodal transportation can be used in (   ) logistics service.
   A. international   B. domestic
   C. middle   D. A and B

Reading Material

Leading Companies Operating in the International Logistics Industry

The leading companies operating in the global logistics industry are specialists in specific areas. For example, UPS and FedEx specialize **specifically** in global parcel delivery. Other companies, such as CEVA Logistics or C.H.Robinson specialize in supply chains and contract ogistics. Other companies have their strengths in global freight forwarding, such as Expeditors International and Panalpina.

Here are brief introductions to several of them:

Chapter 11　International Logistics

1. UPS

UPS is a package delivery company. Every day UPS delivers more than 15 million packages to more than 6.1 million customers in more than 220 countries and **territories** around the world. The company's primary business is the time-definite delivery of packages and documents worldwide. In recent years, it has **extended** its service **portfolio** to include less than truckload transportation (primarily in the U.S.) and supply chain services. UPS reports its operations in three **segments**: U.S. Domestic Package operations, International Package operations, and Supply Chain&Freight operations. U.S. Domestic Package operations include the delivery of letters, documents, and packages throughout the United States. International Package operations includes delivery of letters, documents and packages to more than 220 countries and territories worldwide, as well as shipments from or to the United States with another country as the destination or original point. Supply Chain&Freight consists of its forwarding and logistics operations and other related businesses.

2. FedEx

FedEx Corporation is an American global **courier** delivery services company. It provides a portfolio of transportation, e-commerce and business services under the FedEx brand. The company operates in four segments: FedEx Express, FedEx Ground, FedEx Freight and FedEx Services. Federal Express Corporation (FedEx Express) is an express transportation company, offering time-certain delivery within one to three business days and serving markets. FedEx Ground is a provider of small-package ground delivery service. FedEx Freight is a provider of less-than-truckload (LTL) freight. FedEx Corporate Services, provides its other companies with sales, marketing and information technology support.

3. C.H. Robinson

C.H.Robinson Worldwide, Inc. is one of the world's largest third party logistics providers. The company provides freight transportation services and logistics solutions to companies of all sizes, in a variety of industries. During 2012, C.H.Robinson handled **approximately** 11.5 million shipments and worked with more than 42,000 active customers. It operates through a network of

167

231 offices. As a part of its transportation services, it provides a range of value-added logistics services, such as supply chain consulting and analysis, freight consolidation, core carrier program management, and information reporting. In addition, it offers two other services: sourcing services (Sourcing) and fee-based information services (Information Services). The Sourcing business is the buying, selling, and marketing of fresh produce. The Information Services consisted of its **subsidiary**, T-Chek Systems, Inc. .

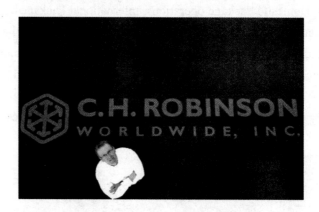

4. Expeditors International

Expeditors International of Washington, Inc. is **engaged** in the business of providing global logistics services. The company offers its customers a network supporting the movement and positioning of goods. Its services include the **consolidation** or forwarding of air and ocean freight. It also acts as a customs broker, and also provides additional services, including distribution management, vendor consolidation, cargo insurance, purchase order management and customized logistics information. During the year ended December 31, 2010, its airfreight services were accounted for 38% of its net revenues; the ocean freight services were accounted for approximately 23% of the company's consolidated revenues, and customs brokerage and other services were accounted for approximately 39% of the company's consolidated net revenues.

【Key Words】

specifically [spəˈsifikli]	adv.	具体地，明确地；按特性地
territory [ˈterətɔːri]	n.	领地，地盘；领域，范围

Chapter 11 International Logistics

extend [ik'stend]	v.	延伸，扩大；推广；提供
portfolio [pɔːt'fəʊliəʊ]	n.	证券投资组合；公文包；代表作品集
segment [seg'ment]	n.	环节；部分，段落；分段
	vt.	分割；划分
courier ['kʊriə(r)]	n.	导游；信使，情报员；通讯员
approximately [ə'prɔksimətli]	adv.	近似，大约地
subsidiary [səb'sidiəri]	n.	附属事物，附属机构；附属者，附属品
	adj.	附带的，附属的，次要的；帮助的；补足的
engage [in'geidʒ]	v.	聘用；吸引；与……交战；参与
consolidation [kən,sɔli'deiʃən]	n.	巩固；合并

【Questions】

1. Why can the companies such as UPS, FedEx be the leading parts in the global logistics industry?
2. Can you give more examples of leading international logistics companies?

Chapter 12
Logistics Business Correspondence

Specimen Letter about Claim for Improper Packing

Dear Sirs,

We refer to Sales Contract No.333 covering the purchase of 200 coffee sets. The **consignment** arrived here on July 22. On examination, we found 16 sets were badly damaged though the packages containing the coffee sets appeared to be in good condition.

Chapter 12 Logistics Business Correspondence

Considering this damage was due to the rough handling by the shipping company, we claimed on them for the loss, but an investigation made by the surveyor has revealed that the damages are **attributable** to improper packing.

On the strength of the survey report, we hereby register our claim against you as follows:

CIF value of 16 sets: US $ 350.00

Inspection fees: US $ 250.00

Total: US $ 600.00

We enclose one copy of survey report No. SR1101 and look forward to your early settlement.

Yours truly,
(Signature)

【Key Words】

consignment [kənˈsainmənt]	n.	装运的货物，托运的货物；托运；托管，委托
attributable [əˈtribjətəbl]	adj.	可归因于……的；由……引起的
signature [ˈsignətʃə(r)]	n.	签名；署名；鲜明特色

Introduction to Logistics Business Correspondence

A business **correspondence** is a letter written in formal language, usually used when writing from one business organization to another, or for correspondence between such organizations and their customer, clients and other external parties. As an important part of business contact, the business letter plays a key role in all kinds of business activities, so does in logistic organizations. Generally speaking, there are nine parts of the logistics business letter as follows: [1]

(1) Heading—heading includes the sender's name, postal address, post code, telephone number, fax number and e-mail address, etc. .

(2) Date—the date line is used to indicate the date the letter is written.

(3) Inside address—the inside address is the recipient's address.

(4) **Salutation**—the most commonly used salutation forms are "Dear Sirs", "Gentlemen" or "Dear Madam".

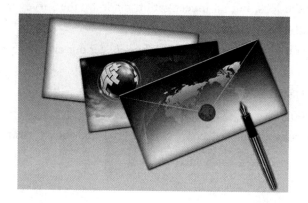

【知识拓展】

(5) Subject line—subject line is actually the central idea of a letter, it is inserted between the salutation and body.

(6) Body—this is the most important part of a letter.

(7) **Complimentary** close—this part is used to provide the letter a courteous.

(8) Signature—the signature is the signed name of the person writing the latter. It is signed by hand in black or blue ink.

(9) **Enclosure**—if it is necessary to enclose any document along with the letter, such as a brochure, attention should be called to it by writing "Enclosure", "Enclosures" or " Encl.", below the signature in the lower left-hand corner.

Specimen Letter

Allen Incorporation
1470 St. Louis Street
Los Angeles, CA 90015
U. S. A.
March 15, 2015

China National Import & Export Corp.
Shanghai Branch
Shanghai
China

Subject: Order No. 8 for Tools

Gentlemen,

This is to inform you that Mr. White, **president** of ABC logistics Inc. **resigned** from that company and **established** a new company under the name of Allen Inc..[2] We are pleased to place with you our first trial order as enclosed, which we hope, would lead to good business relations between our two companies.[3]

Please fax your sales **confirmation** with net price on CIF Los Angeles basis. [4]

We are looking forwards to replying sooner.

Yours sincerely
Allen Inc.
James Smith
(Signature)

Chapter 12　Logistics Business Correspondence

【Key Words】

correspondence [ˌkɔrəˈspɔndəns]	n.	信件，函电；通信；关联
salutation [ˌsæljuˈteiʃn]	n.	招呼；致意；信函中的称呼语
complimentary [ˌkɔmpliˈmentəri]	adj.	表示敬意的；赞美的；赠送的
enclosure [inˈkləuʒə(r)]	n.	围场；圈地；（信）附件
president [ˈprezidənt]	n.	总统；总裁；院长；主席
resign [riˈzain]	v.	辞职；放弃；屈从
establish [iˈstæbliʃ]	vt.	创建，建立；成立；证实
confirmation [ˌkɔnfəˈmeiʃn]	n.	证实，证据；确认书

【Notes to Text A】

[1] Generally speaking, there are nine parts of the logistics business letter as follows.

物流商务信函的9个部分为：信头（heading）、日期（date）、信内地址（inside address）、称呼（salutation）、事由（subject line）、正文（body）、结束敬语（complimentary close）、签名（signature）和附件（enclosure）。

[2] This is to inform you that Mr. White, president of ABC logistics Inc. resigned from that company and established a new company under the name of Allen Inc..

在国际商务活动中，常见的职衔如下：

president, chairman	总裁，董事长
general manager	总经理
deputy general manager	副总经理
executive vice president	执行副总裁
HR manager	人力资源经理
project manager	项目经理
logistics manager	物流经理
sourcing director	采购主管

[3] We are pleased to place with you our first trial order as enclosed, which we hope, would lead to good business relations between our two companies.

短语"to place with you our first trial order"中介词"with"提前，常见的短语为"to place an order with sb."（向某人）订货，例如：

to place a trial order with sb.	（向某人）试订货
to place a repeat order with sb.	（向某人）继续订货
to place a substantial order with sb.	（向某人）大批订货

句中"which"引导非限制性定语从句。

[4] Please fax your sales confirmation with net price on CIF Los Angeles basis.

在商务活动中表示价格的词组与贸易术语：

(1) 一些常见表示价格的词组。

net price	净价
lowest price	最低价

reasonable price	合理价
prevailing price	现行价

(2) CIF 为国际贸易术语，常见的 6 个国际贸易术语。

EXW (Ex Works)	工厂交货
FCA (Free Carrier)	货交承运人
FAS (Free Alongside Ship)	船边交货
FOB (Free on Board)	船上交货
CFR (Cost and Fright)	成本加运费
CIF (Cost, Insurance and Freight)	成本、保险和运费

【Exercises to Text A】

I. Fill in the blanks.

1. This is to inform you that Mr. White, president of ABC logistics Inc. resigned _____ that company and established a new company under the name of Allen Inc. .

2. We are pleased to place with you our first _____ order as enclosed.

3. Please fax your sales _____ with net price on CIF Los Angeles basis.

4. Our quotation _____ 20 tons of Shandong groundnuts is valid for 10 days.

5. Please extend your L/C to August 15 and August 31 _____ shipment and negotiation respectively.

II. Translation.

1. 我方现附寄一份价格单，供你方参考。

2. 如你方需要进一步的信息资料，请传真给我们。

3. 我是物流公司的采购主管，希望向贵公司大量订货，以此建立两公司的业务关系。

4. 我在一家零售商负责供应链管理，这家零售商有 150 个零售店、2 个配送中心，我的任务是在今后的 5 年里建立一个最佳供应链，以满足顾客的需求。

III. Writing.

1. Read this part of a letter your boss has received from Ms. Miller, a conference organizer.

I am writing to ask if you would attend a seminar on 27 March and give a speech on business issues.

Chapter 12　Logistics Business Correspondence

Accommodations and the use of a car will be provided.

If you could come, please confirm the subject of your speech and standard of accommodations you would need.

I am looking forward to hearing from you.

Your boss has asked you to reply to the letter.

2. Write a letter to Ms. Miller.

The letter should include the following points:

(1) Accepting the invitation.

(2) Giving out the subject of your boss's speech.

(3) Explaining why your boss is interested in this subject.

(4) Reserving a hotel room.

Write about 150 words.

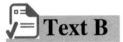 Text B

Establishing Business Relations

A letter to establish business relations is a piece of writing to find and **negotiate** with a new business partner, it is the first step for a logistics company to expand its business.[1] In order to enter into business relations, a logistics company will find the **channels** as followings to obtain a new customer's the name and address:

(1) The bank.

(2) The **chamber** of **commerce**.

(3) The **Commercial Counselor's Office**.

(4) The fair.

(5) Introduction carried on by friend.

(6) Advertisement.

> **Specimen Letter**
>
> Dear Sirs,
>   We have obtained your name and address from the Commercial Counsellor's Office of your embassy in London and are now writing you for the establishment of business relations. [2]
>   We are a very famous logistics Co., Ltd. in China and are willing to **act as** your **forwarding** or shipping agent as well as the agency carrying stock. [3] We would like to work with you to market them here. Our **reference** is the Bank of China in China. They can provide you with information about our business and finance.
>   We are looking forward to your early reply.
>
>   Yours sincerely
>   Lucy

【Key Words】

negotiate [nɪˈɡəʊʃɪeɪt]	vi.	谈判，协商；洽谈，交涉
	vt.	谈判达成；议价出售
channel [ˈtʃænl]	n.	海峡；通道；渠道，途径；频道
chamber [ˈtʃeɪmbə(r)]	n.	房间；会议厅，会所；议会
commerce [ˈkɒmɜːs]	n.	贸易；商业
Commercial Counselor's Office		商务参赞处
act as		担任
forward [ˈfɔːwəd]	adv.	向前，前进；提前
	adj.	向前方的，向前进的；预约的
	vt.	发送；转交；促进
	n.	（足球、曲棍球等的）前锋
reference [ˈrefrəns]	n.	参考，参考书目；提及；推荐信；介绍人
	v.	引用
	adj.	供参考的

【Notes to Text B】

[1] A letter to establish business relations is a piece of writing to find and negotiate with a new business partner. It is the first step for a logistics company to expand its business.

"to find and negotiate with a new business partner" 动词不定式作定语。

"it" 为指示代词，代替 "a letter to establish business relations"。

[2] We have obtained your name and address from the Commercial Counsellor's Office of your embassy in London and are now writing you for the establishment of business relations.

"to obtain one's name and address from" 意为 "由某处得知某人的姓名和地址"。

还可以表示为：

Chapter 12　Logistics Business Correspondence

to have/learn /know one's name and address from…
to owe one's name and address to…
to obtain one's name and address through (by) courtesy of…
"to establish business relations with…" 意为"和……建立商务关系"。
还可表示为"to enter into business relations with…",例如:
We are willing to establish business relations with you on the basis of equality and mutual benefit. 我们愿在平等互利的基础上与贵方建立商务关系。

[3] We are a very famous logistics Co., Ltd. in China and are willing to act as your forwarding or shipping agent as well as the agency carrying stock.

(1) 表示公司和企业的专用词组。

Co., Ltd.	有限公司
a multi-national corporation	跨国公司
a joint venture	合资企业
a state-owned enterprise	国有企业
a foreign capital enterprise	外资企业

(2) 物流公司承担的代理。

forwarding or shipping agent	运输代理
agency carrying stock	仓储代理
international freighter forwarder	国际货运代理

【Exercises to Text B】

I. Fill in the blanks.

1. We are a very famous state-owned enterprise _____.
从网上得知贵公司的地址和名称,我方愿和你方建立贸易关系。
2. We are given to understand that _____.
贵公司有意在平等互利的基础上与我公司建立业务关系。
3. We take liberty to write to _____.
请求担任你方在中国的运输代理。
4. We should be greatly obliged _____.
如能尽快航寄贵公司有关价格的详细资料。
5. We are glad to inform you that _____.
我方能够提供各项售后服务以满足贵方需要。

II. Reading and answering questions.

Ocean freight rates may be broadly divided into tramp rates and liner freight rates. Tramp rates fluctuate with the market conditions of supply and demand. In a boom period, the tramp rates rise; in a period of recession, they decline. Liner freight rates are fixed by shipping conferences and other liner operations. They are related more to the costs of operation that remain comparatively steady over a period time.

Freight forwarders are mainly concerned with liner freight rates. Although the principles on which the liner freight rates are fixed have not been clarified by shipping conferences or operations, it is evident that the cost of providing such services will cover actual cost and a margin of profit. The total cost of providing such services consist of fixed costs and variable costs. Fixed costs include costs, interest, and depreciation. Variable costs involve cost of fuel, loading and unloading expenses, and port costs.

When determining the freight rate, a carrier will also consider the stowage factor, distance, And the age-old principle of what the traffic can bear.

In fact, the principle of what the traffic can bear in effect means that commodities that are highly rated subsidize those that are rated lower. This principle was more commonly adopted in the past than the cost of service principle because of the problems involved in the computation of the actual unit costs. However, containerization with standardized cargo units has made the calculation of the service cost per unit easier than heterogeneous break bulk cargoes. The carriers are therefore increasingly adopting the service cost principle nowadays, particularly with a view to fighting competition.

Open market rates are also taken into account. When commodities are moved in large quantities and are susceptible to charter competition, the rates may be left "open" so that a liner has the option of charging whatever is considered appropriate in the competitive situation.

Liner rates are also subject to surcharges or adjustment factors that may be levied from time to time in order to enable the shipping lines to meet certain price variations in their inputs such as a currency adjustment factor (CAF), a bunker adjustment factor (BAF), and port congestion surcharges.

Container freight rates generally include charges for inland haulage and terminal charges at the port of loading and port of discharging. There are different types of container freight rates.

Commodity Box Rates (CBR) is a lump sum rate for the carriage of a container loaded with a particular commodity. The rate is based on the average utilization of the box. For the carrier, the rate simplifies calculations and reduces administrative costs. Large shippers prefer CBR for particular voyages, but it is not suitable for small shippers.

Freight All Kinds (FAK) Rates is the alternative to the commodity box rate and is based on the principle that what goes into the container is irrelevant to the freight which should be charged. In other words, all commodities are charged the same rate for the same voyage regardless of their value. The FAK rate is logical since it is the container that is loaded and unloaded and occupies space on hand a vessel.

Questions:

1. Which of the following statements are true about liner freight rates? (   )

    A. They fluctuate with market conditions of supply and demand.

    B. Liner freight rates are fixed by shipping conferences and other liner operator.

Chapter 12 Logistics Business Correspondence

    C. They are related more to the costs of operation.

    D. Freight forwarders are mainly concerned with tramp rates.

2. What do fixed costs include? (　　)

    A. cost of officers and crew

    B. insurance, repairs and maintenance

    C. cost of fuel, loading and unloading expense

    D. administrative costs, interest, and depreciation

3. Which of the following do variable costs involve? (　　)

    A. administrative costs   B. cost of officers and crew

    B. cost of fuel   D. loading and unloading expenses

4. Line rates are also subject to surcharges or adjustment factors such as (　　).

    A. currency adjustment factor   B. port congestion surcharges

    C. bunker adjustment factor   D. stowage factor

5. Which of the following are true about Commodity Box Rates? (　　)

    A. All commodities are charged the same rate for the same voyage regardless of their value.

    B. It simplifies calculations and reduces administrative costs.

    C. The rate is based on the average utilization of the box.

    D. It is a lump sum rate for the carriage of a container loaded with a particular commodity.

III. Translation.

我方 2020 年 8 月 12 日第 188 号函，曾请你报来运输电冰箱的报价。如果你方尚未发出该项报价单，请尽快航寄。事实上，我方现已收到其他供货人的报价单。出于对你方的考虑，请速报，以免失去合作机会。

如贵方能利用这一时机，为双方的合作铺平道路，则我们之间的贸易前景是十分广阔的。

IV. Writing.

1. Read this part of a letter from Mr. White, a conference organizer.

We have pleasure in inviting you to our annual conference to be held at the Hilton Hotel here in Los Angeles, from 10 to 15 October, 2020.

Details of the conference, accommodation arrangements and a provisional program have been enclosed.

Last year you gave a very interesting presentation on the subject of "Major Principles of Logistical Management". We would be very grateful if you could consider giving us an update on this.

Please confirm your participation at your earliest convenience.

2. Write a letter to Mr. White.

The letter should include the following points:

(1) Referring to the invitation.

(2) Confirming your participation.

(3) Requesting more information about the program.

(4) Apologizing and giving reasons for not being able to give another presentation.

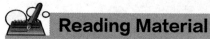

Response to Complaints and Claims

Excellent service is a vital factor for a logistics company to gain success, however, sometimes the customers may complain and claim for improper packing, late delivery or inferior quality, etc.. How will you respond to the customers' complaints and claims?

Specimen Letter

Dear Sirs,

Thank you for your letter of 22 June, 2015. Your complaint and claim about shortage of 3 boxes has been noted.

We have contacted our forwarding agent who informs us that your three boxes were **over-carried** and landed in Shenyang.

We are making arrangements to have the three boxes of tape recorders returned to Tianjin by the first available **opportunity** and we will bear any charges and expenses thus incurred.

As to the cables you referred to for **computer-connection**, they can be provide as an optional extra and were not quoted to you. In this instance, due to the **misunderstanding**, we would be please to provide you at no charge, and you will have them together with the next shipment under the **S/C** No. BP 188.

Please accept our apologies for the inconvenience caused to you.

Yours truly,
(Signature)

【Key Words】

over-carried	n.	过运；超载
opportunity [ˌɔpəˈtjuːnəti]	n.	机会，良机；有利的环境
computer-connection	n.	计算机连接
misunderstanding [ˌmisʌndəˈstændiŋ]	n.	误解，误会；争执
S/C		Sales Confirmation 的缩写，即销售合同

【Questions】

What is the best way when dealing with complaints from customers?